VACATION RENTAL MASTERY

**Beyond Airbnb: high occupancy,
direct bookings & serious money**

REX BROWN

Zen Insights Publishing
6 Sarsfield St
Separation Creek,
Victoria Australia 3234

Copyright © Rex Brown 2018

ISBN: 978-0-9876357-0-9
eISBN: 978-0-9876357-1-6

First published in 2018 by Zen Insights Publishing

Editing: Tony Ryan
Cover design: Peter Long
Text design and layout: Lorna Hendry

To Sibylle

Contents

PART 1: Key Ideas   1

CHAPTER 1: The Turbulent Vacation Rental World   2
CHAPTER 2: Our Story   6
CHAPTER 3: Your Goals   11
CHAPTER 4: The Big Gorillas   13
CHAPTER 5: Using This Book For High Occupancy   18
CHAPTER 6: Roadmap To Success   23
CHAPTER 7: Mindset   29

PART 2: Basics For High Occupancy   31

CHAPTER 8: Best Website Listings   32
CHAPTER 9: Excellent Photographs   38
CHAPTER 10: Accurate Calendar And Pricing   46
CHAPTER 11: A Name That Stands Out   51
CHAPTER 12: A Description That Stands Out   55
CHAPTER 13: A Seamless Cleaning Process   62
CHAPTER 14: The Organized Back Office   65
CHAPTER 15: Risk Management   68
CHAPTER 16: A Great Guest Experience   73
CHAPTER 17: The Basics Quiz   78

PART 3: Advanced Techniques For Mastery   83

CHAPTER 18: The VRM Advanced Techniques Matrix   84

SECTION 1: Human Motivation   89

CHAPTER 19: Customer Feedback Obsession   90

CHAPTER 20: The Psychology Of Influence   96

CHAPTER 21: Standing Out With A Theme   110

SECTION 2: Core Processes For Mastery   119

CHAPTER 22: Loyalty System   120

CHAPTER 23: Guest Newsletter—Examples   128

CHAPTER 24: Guest Newsletter—Choosing A System   138

CHAPTER 25: Guest Newsletter—Maximizing Readership   146

CHAPTER 26: Your Own Website—Why You Need It   154

CHAPTER 27: Your Own Website—Choosing An Approach   160

CHAPTER 28: Your Own Website—What's On It?   170

CHAPTER 29: Online Booking Capability   174

CHAPTER 30: Your Google "My Business" Listing   177

SECTION 3: Tactical Advantages   185

CHAPTER 31: Conversion Tactics   186

CHAPTER 32: Last-minute Levers To Pull   193

CHAPTER 33: Guest Reviews   195

CHAPTER 34: Understanding And Exploiting The Big Four   202

CHAPTER 35: Optimizing For Airbnb   210

CHAPTER 36: Optimizing For HomeAway   216

CHAPTER 37: Optimizing For Booking.com   220

CHAPTER 38: Optimizing For TripAdvisor   225

CHAPTER 39: Optimizing Your Prices   227

CHAPTER 40: Search Engine Optimization   230

CHAPTER 41: Insiders' Expert Guides   234

CHAPTER 42: Google Ads   238

CHAPTER 43: Managed Services   242

SECTION 4: High Value-Add Extras   245

CHAPTER 44: Knowledge Sources   246

CHAPTER 45: Mastermind   250

CHAPTER 46: Publicity   255

CHAPTER 47: Offline Marketing   257

CHAPTER 48: Social Media   260

CHAPTER 49: Facebook Ads   263

CHAPTER 50: Channel Managers   265

CHAPTER 51: Tips And Hacks   268

CHAPTER 52: The Advanced Quiz   275

CHAPTER 53: Conclusion—Continuing The Journey   279

REFERENCES   280

SPECIAL SYMBOLS

These are used to highlight key concepts (see page 21)

 Barriers to entry

 Using psychology for bookings

 Ways to get direct bookings

PART 1

KEY IDEAS

In this part, I describe the turbulent environment of the vacation rental industry. It is rapidly changing, and is becoming dominated by a few large multinational corporations.

Despite all this, small vacation rental owners can succeed and achieve outstanding results, as shown by my own story.

The Roadmap To Success charts the path that will help you succeed in a few short years, provided you have the right mindset. The rest of the book shows you how.

CHAPTER 1

The Turbulent Vacation Rental World

All around the world, owners of second houses or apartments are renting them out to travelers who want to enjoy a vacation rental[1] experience, living in someone else's house as if it were their own. Many are part of the Airbnb phenomenon, the sharing economy.

For some owners, renting out their house is a mystery, with a poor return. For others with the right knowledge it is a very profitable business, where they can make serious money. That is what this book is about—giving owners the knowledge and skills to achieve exceptional bookings and make serious money.

> Knowledge is the difference between a struggling vacation rental and serious money.

In many markets, casual owners may take $10,000 a year total rental[2] while they are occupied just 10% of the time, but those achieving mastery **with similar properties** can achieve 90% occupancy and over $100,000—serious money. In some markets with

---

[1] By "vacation rental" in this book, I mean some kind of short-term standalone accommodation that travelers can use for vacations or holidays. It can include B&Bs and condos, but it generally excludes hotels, motels. Abbreviation is VR.

[2] Throughout this book, references to amounts of money are in US dollars unless otherwise specified.

high starting rental rates, the numbers double. Knowledge is the difference between low and full occupancy.

This is a book for vacation rental owners, written by a vacation rental owner with over 20 years experience. I've written this book so you don't have to wait years before achieving 80%–90% occupancy. It explains how most folks can run their vacation rentals **exceptionally** well and achieve vacation rental mastery—the title of this book.

Although we may be small individually, there are around 5 million vacation rentals around the globe, more than you might expect, and that number is growing fast. Business Wire (2017) report that the global vacation rental market will be worth around $194 billion by 2019. That is more than the economy of many small countries.

Enterprising folks around the world are finding they can earn enough from short-term vacation rental to finance the ownership of their own vacation home. Similarly, vacation houses that used to sit idle are now earning major incomes while still allowing their owners to enjoy fabulous vacations when they like. Retired owners of vacation rentals are enjoying a lifestyle that is personally rewarding and bringing them income that they never thought possible.

This change in the use of vacation homes globally has been made possible by the magic of the internet, which allows a wonderful house or apartment anywhere to be discovered by folks anywhere who are willing to pay for the privilege of staying.

A few years ago, not many travelers around the world were aware of the benefits of staying in a vacation rental compared to a hotel.

Thanks to the Airbnb publicity machine, VR awareness increased from around 15% in 2015 to around 80% in 2017 (Ting 2017; Shakespeare 2016). More people than ever stay in vacation rentals.

Travelers have discovered they can enjoy the character of a large house or a spacious apartment with far more facilities than a hotel. They can cook for themselves. They can stretch out and enjoy the privacy of their own space without being pestered by hotel staff. They can live like a local, and they can discover the charm and character of a rental that is different from any other.

It is a win for both owners and travelers.

Online travel agencies like Airbnb and HomeAway have made it easier for inexperienced owners to get started in a few hours and have their vacation rental advertised to travelers around the world, often taking bookings within the next few days. But there is more to it than that.

Incredible variation of vacation rental outcomes

While the tools available through the big listing sites make it easy to get started running a vacation rental, the results vary dramatically depending on the skills of the owner. There are many different stories.

Some owners can take years to get their VR occupied for only six months in a year. Others in seasonal markets with summer holidays can be fully occupied for six weeks and mostly empty the rest of the year.

> In general, nights rented as a proportion of nights available in the year = occupancy. **Vacation rental mastery targets occupancy around 90% of nights in a year.**

In very hot markets, where demand outstrips supply, skilled owners with a short-term rental can be quickly well occupied—enough to finance a second short-term rental. However, in the same very hot markets, overly rapid change can trigger regulation that puts the same successful owners out of business overnight.

It has already happened in Paris, New York and Barcelona and is happening in many more locations, like Sydney. Savvy owners are aware of this and take care where they invest.

For some owners, it is a hard business, and they struggle to make more than a tiny return. For others, like me, VRs are rented around 90% of the year, and it is a very good business.

Knowledge is the difference

How is it that one owner can struggle and another can earn serious money in the same market? The difference is knowledge, and applying that knowledge.

That is the reason this book was written—to share knowledge with vacation rental owners around the world and help them succeed.

From long experience I have found that to be successful a vacation rental owner should get the basics right first, then use more advanced techniques to drive more bookings and get high occupancy. It is the simple model I have used when speaking to VR owners at several Stayz (HomeAway's predecessor) conferences.

> **Basics + Advanced = High Occupancy**

After the introductory ideas, this book is structured into those two parts: Basics and Advanced.

CHAPTER 2

Our Story

In the 1990s my wife, Sibylle, bought a small vacation house called Treetops in the coastal village of Wye River, three hours away from where we lived in Melbourne, Australia.

We both worked in corporate roles and understood the emerging power of the internet and how it could energize our vacation rental. I came from a background in engineering and customer service and was managing web applications. Sibylle came from a knowledge management background after taking a major newspaper online. She also had a strong sense of style and strategy. Our skills would complement each other in taking Treetops to high levels of occupancy. We would jointly work on design, and I would run the operation, as we did for all three of our VRs.

We used a local manager to run the house for us remotely, but we drove inquiries and bookings. We experimented with the look, the theme, the layout, and the marketing. We added a website and used Google Ads to drive traffic. We deconstructed the Stayz site on which we advertised. We deciphered the listing site promotion system and used it to push Treetops to the top of listings.

We made many mistakes along the way. One was using oddments of furniture to save money, but we noticed that it gave the place a sad, neglected feel, so we freshened it up and updated the furniture. It became instantly appealing to guests, and bookings steadily grew.

Another mistake I made was to half-heartedly tinker with a newsletter that went out twice in two years to past guests and never gained traction. In later years I was to turn our newsletter to a powerful storytelling and marketing tool that was appreciated by past guests.

In time, the locals noticed that little Treetops, with three bedrooms, seemed to always have a different car in the driveway. There was often smoke from the chimney when most other houses stayed idle in the cold winter season. In the brief summer season, most houses were booked, and most returned to idle when the peak two months ended. Treetops stayed rented 80% of the year.

We were asked what we were doing differently and ran a few internet marketing workshops, but otherwise kept to ourselves.

When we changed houses in inner Melbourne in 2006, we rented our three-bedroom house short-term rather than selling, and again we found we were occupied over 80% of the time, far more than our competition. I realized we had a special way of operating that worked in different markets. Some experiments didn't work, like Google Ads in a commodity market. Others worked, like local letterbox drops for visiting families in urban areas.

Accidental discovery of a huge market gap

In 2006 we took our two dogs on a 3,000-kilometer road trip to northern Australia. Finding nice places to stay with dogs was almost impossible. We were prepared to pay well above the market rate, but there were no places available. We checked our local market and found the same gap—a poor supply of premium pet-friendly rentals. It was our light bulb moment, and from then on we worked to capitalize on the opportunity. Soon pet owners were half our guests.

Our gamble

In 2010 we decided to take a calculated risk—leave the corporate world, make a sea change to Wye River, and build a permanent house there with a vacation rental attached.

We designed the new rental around our customers, young couples who wanted comfort but also somewhere special they could bring their pet dog. We chose a Japanese theme, and "Sea Zen," our luxury rental with extra pampering facilities, was the vision. We tried concepts on friends and family. We had open debates on placement of the spa. We took a deep breath and designed and built it.

We tapped into everything we had learned in the prior 10 years. We decorated it around our unique Zen theme. I painstakingly crafted a simple welcome book that gave guests easy tips to make their stay effortless. I put in a guestbook and a guest questionnaire.

I built a website, placed ads on the best online travel agencies, drove high placement. I took more risks placing expensive Google ads targeting pet lovers.

But would it work?

First misgivings

The first booking in 2012 was not great—the plumber accidentally turned off the treatment plant and the smell was horrible for a day, but luckily the wind blew in the right direction. The first guests left saying nothing. We were nervous that we had miscalculated the market.

The next guest, Meredith, arrived early while we were still cleaning. She ran up the stairs, looked around, flung out her arms and said, "Yes, yes, yes. Wow!" She had been looking for an apartment like ours for design inspiration and Sea Zen hit the mark. We let out a long breath. We were in business. She and her family came back six times in the next few years.

Within three months all the marketing kicked in, and Sea Zen was running at 90% occupancy and has stayed that way since. Our newsletter kept in touch with past guests.

I kept obsessively listening to our guests and kept adding tiny touches they asked for. I experimented and sometimes failed, like when I put in a fridge with local wines that nobody used. Our romantic package flopped. Other experiments worked, like arranging the spa screens so the to the indoor spa could be converted to an outdoor spa.

Guests loved our local food guide. I drove up the number of guest reviews. With 90% occupancy, I kept creeping prices up and soon we were well above the market rate.

Disaster stress testing

In 2015, bushfires destroyed 118 of 340 houses in our village, including our Treetops rental. Sea Zen was untouched, but there was immense brand damage to the village—most travelers didn't want to stay where there had been a bad fire. Our systems kicked in as we connected to past loyal guests via the newsletter and Sea Zen kept running full.

In 2016, rain and landslips closed the one road through town—more brand damage. Again, Sea Zen kept running full due to loyal guests.

In 2017, I was flattened with illness, but Sibylle took bookings and the automated systems kept working. Sea Zen kept running full. In 2018, while I fought the illness, Airbnb doubled our competition in town, making bookings harder, but Sea Zen kept running full. Our systems kept working.

What we do is not unique. All around the world there are thousands of owners who have experimented and succeeded. Over time they have acquired the knowledge on how to succeed in the complex, changing world of vacation rentals. They have unconsciously achieved *vacation rental mastery.*

This book is designed to help you get the knowledge quickly, so you too can succeed, but without years of learning in a changing environment. It also teaches how to combat the "big gorillas"—the online travel agencies (OTAs)—and get more direct bookings.

> This book is designed to help you acquire the key knowledge to maximize bookings and returns quickly

CHAPTER 3

Your Goals

What are your goals as a VR owner?

A. Lifestyle/hobby

You can have a fulfilling life running a VR. How hard you run it and the results you achieve are up to you, but a relaxed operation will give modest returns.

B. Investment

For some, the higher returns from a VR are seen as an easy path to riches compared to long-term rental, accelerated by hard deals and win/lose relationships. Nothing is further from the truth. It takes long-term effort and good relationships to achieve lasting results.

C. Small business entrepreneur

Running your own VR as a business can be rewarding and enjoyable, particularly if you love helping other people.

> This book is written for the small business entrepreneur who wants to get the maximum return from their VR business while enjoying helping other people, their guests

Do you need to start your own vacation rental?

This book is targeted at readers who already own their own vacation rental. If you are interested in investing and starting from the beginning, this book is not for you. Go to Holidayrentalmastery.com for free tips and resources on starting.

Knowledge is key to revenue

Over my 20 years of experience in the VR industry, I have countless times seen that identical vacation rentals can earn a huge range of incomes, depending on the knowledge and skills of the owner.

In my research into typical returns from VRs, I developed a model of a typical two-bedroom VR operating in a vacation area. I found that net revenues of $13,000, $65,000, and $115,000 are all possible outcomes from the same property, **depending on how the owner manages it**. This is a staggering but realistic range! **This book helps you move to the upper levels.**

RENTAL RETURNS CAN BE RADICALLY DIFFERENT AND ARE DOMINATED BY OWNER SKILLS AND EFFORT.

$13,000	$65,000	$115,000
Low skills, remote managed	Average skills	Advanced skills and involvement, onsite cleaning

CHAPTER 4

The Big Gorillas

The environment we small VR owners operate in is dominated by a few very large online travel agencies. You will have heard of them and have probably used them—Airbnb, HomeAway VRBO, Booking.com and TripAdvisor. While Airbnb is a stand-alone, HomeAway and VRBO are owned by the hotel booking giant Expedia, and Booking.com is owned by the hotel booking giant Booking Holdings.

These very big gorillas are skilled at using the internet at scale. They have easy systems for owners to list and for travelers to use. They aggressively buy Google ads in every market in the world to attract travelers. They spend millions on TV ads. They have corporate publicity campaigns. Their brands are well known. They are the easiest places for travelers to book holidays. They deliver bookings to VR owners, but inevitably over time they have been increasing their commissions and squeezing VR owner margins.

The great game—where we can win!

While the online travel agency gorillas dominate with the unfair advantage of scale, we VR owners have our own unfair advantage. **We have a relationship, a unique intimacy with our guests that no OTA can match.** We can build guest loyalty based on that intimacy. We can also be the go-to local experts in our own market.

The great game is for OTAs to keep guests for themselves, while we VR owners need to embrace guests into our personal loyalty schemes. We will revisit the loyalty theme many times in later chapters.

The strategy for VR owners is also to have our own systems so our reliance on the OTA listing sites drops over time. Our core tactic is to retain loyal guests.

The Airbnb phenomenon

Many owners have a love–hate relationship with Airbnb. I have an enormous respect for Airbnb—and a wary distrust.

Airbnb started with the flaky idea of renting airbeds in spare rooms of homes. The founders are obsessed with designing around customers' needs and rapidly evolved a unique system to allow travelers to find hosts. Although the rhetoric of their story mesmerized journalists by saying they are creating a sharing economy and just renting out spare space, the reality is far more complicated.

In reality, they are facilitating short-term rentals like their competitors. But they have invented a better mousetrap and are doing it better. They quickly understood that the key to travelers renting is to have **strong trust** between the parties, and their systems deliver on that. There are at least six layers of trust:

- Guests review hosts like other online travel agencies so guests can *trust* the host, but the Airbnb twist is for hosts to review guests, so the hosting owners can assess the risk of renting to and *trusting* unknown travelers.
- Money is handled by Airbnb, so there is *trusted* financial security for guests and hosts.
- Airbnb also has a $1 million damage guarantee (with strings in the fine print) so hosts can *trust* that they won't be financially ruined by a wild party.
- Airbnb in the early days provided free professional photographs so guests could *trust* that the property would be as described.

- There is a help service so both parties can *trust* they have someone to help them if something goes wrong.

The processes are as frictionless as possible. The sign-up process is simple, with helpful prompts for the new host to fill in the blanks. The booking engine has useful filters for location and price to make booking easy for guests. During the stay, the system prompts both parties, so the guest has an easy welcome with good information, and after the stay both parties are prompted to make reviews.

Good hosts are rewarded for good experiences, becoming "superhosts." Both hosts and guests are rewarded financially for referrals, helping to drive viral growth.

Airbnb's better mousetrap has driven astonishing growth. While they started small, soon they grew dramatically at over 100% compound per year!

Their main competitor, HomeAway, had over five years grown by acquisition and a little organic growth and in the early years were dominant. They were disdainful of Airbnb as "just sharing rooms for young millennials." As they were stalked and overtaken by Airbnb, they took the threat seriously. In 2018, they capitulated, and transformed their systems to a near clone of Airbnb's!

This graph of the growth in listings by Airbnb and HomeAway, based on data from Hinote (2015) and others below, shows the exponential growth in Airbnb outstripping HomeAway.

GROWTH IN PROPERTY LISTINGS

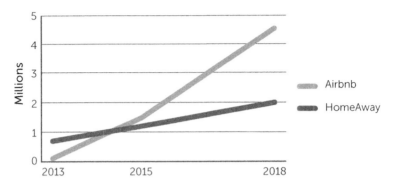

Size comparisons

Airbnb in early 2018 listed over 4.5 million properties globally in 65,000 cities and 191 countries (Jones 2018). HomeAway listed 2 million properties in 190 countries. (HomeAway 2018). Booking.com claimed 5 million rooms (Schaal 2018).

The fuzzy definition of "vacation rental" makes it difficult to compare actual VR numbers between companies.

Some realities of Airbnb

Of course, in exchange for its ease of use and bookings provided to the VR owner, Airbnb charges fees. A confusing two-part fee translates to a hefty 15% more for guests than booking directly with an owner.

Airbnb intentionally keeps control of the guest's identity so owners and guests cannot communicate freely. The VR property brand name is also effectively masked so the guest finds it hard to remember, and this combination of concealment makes it hard for guests to return. In later chapters I explain how you can turn this to your advantage.

Many analysts have found that new owner "hosts" just starting out are given encouragement by Airbnb via high rankings in the early weeks so they quickly get new bookings, a bit like an immediate jackpot from a gambling machine that keeps the gambler gambling for years. For the new hosts, the quick bookings tail off, but the hope and enthusiasm endure.

Problems have also resulted from the astonishing growth rate of Airbnb. Cities have found that a small number of short-term rentals one year have expanded in a few years later to many thousands, soaking up local housing for workers and changing the character of neighborhoods too quickly. In frustration, many cities have changed the rules and some cities like New York and Barcelona have banned most short-term rentals. Even San Francisco the home of Airbnb has banned most short-term rentals. Enthusiastic owners can go from a very busy rental to being out of business overnight.

The practical impact for all VR owners is that the astonishing growth of Airbnb has increased competition in our local markets dramatically. Airbnb tells hosts that they should start with low prices until they have good reviews. They also tell hosts that average prices are lower, suggesting prices be dropped. The net result is a flood of low-priced competition for other owners. This is good for travelers wanting cheap accommodation.

> If you are not careful, you will be reduced to renting your gorgeous vacation rental as a cut-price Airbnb commodity

Standing out

Later chapters explain how you can turn this commoditization to your advantage by **standing out** from the crowd. The extra attention gets you more bookings and more income.

CHAPTER 5

Using This Book For High Occupancy

At its simplest, you need to focus on the few things to get your **basics** right, then focus on the few things to get your **advanced** systems right. If successful, you can achieve occupancy of around 90%.

> Basic techniques + advanced techniques = high occupancy

That is how this book is structured after this introduction:
- The second part deals with basic techniques.
- The third part deals with advanced techniques.

Of course, I walk you through each of the steps to make it easy. You take it in the order you choose.

What are these basics?

I devote a whole section of this book to basics. They are important because without them you are unlikely to get 10% occupancy, let alone 90%!

In the Basics section I will cover:
- best website listing
- excellent photographs
- accurate calendar and pricing

- a name that stands out
- a description that stands out
- a seamless cleaning process
- the organized back office
- risk management
- a great guest experience
- a quiz that provides a reality check.

What are the advanced steps?

Motivation

This is core to everything else that follows in the advanced steps. Those who believe they can succeed will; those who believe it is too hard will find it too hard.

Topics:
- customer feedback obsession
- using the psychology of influence
- standing out with a theme.

Core processes

This is the machinery that you will put in place that takes you to the next level.

Topics:
- loyalty system
- guest newsletter
- your own website
- online booking capability
- Google's "My Business" listings.

Tactical advantages

These are the tactics that, with attention to detail, will help you optimize opportunities.

Topics:
- conversion tactics

- last-minute levers to pull
- guest reviews
- understanding and exploiting the big four online travel agencies
- optimizing each of the big four
- optimizing your prices
- search engine optimization (SEO)
- insiders' expert guides
- Google Ads
- managed services.

High value-add extras

These are the icing on the cake that help you find opportunities that others won't see.

Topics:
- knowledge sources you can use
- mastermind groups
- publicity
- offline marketing
- social media
- Facebook ads
- channel managers
- tips and hacks
- a quiz that provides a reality check.

Recommended tools

Along the way I show you various software tools and products to make your journey easier, some of which I strongly endorse. As a clear disclaimer, I am not paid by any business for endorsement of these products.

Key concept—barriers to entry

There is a harsh story of two travelers lost in the jungle who see a wild tiger bearing down on them. "We'll be eaten; we can't run faster than the tiger," says one. "No, you'll be eaten; I can run faster than you," says the other.

Sometimes it is about getting ahead of your competition.

Some steps on the journey to improving your VR will be harder than others. A theme I will revisit is that some of the harder steps are a small obstacle if you have the right information, and when you do get through them you are ahead of your competitors. Where examples of barriers to entry are discussed you will see the small symbol beside the example.

> Barriers to entry are wonderful; they can be passed with knowledge, then they give you an advantage over your competitors.

Key concept—psychology of influence

A new concept developed later in this book and rarely discussed in our industry shows how certain psychological triggers change people's behavior, and how this "psychology of influence" can help you get more bookings. Where examples of this are discussed, you will see a small symbol beside the examples.

Key concept—direct bookings

Using the online travel agencies will only get you so far. To get high occupancy with low commission fees, you will also need to take more direct bookings yourself. Many of the techniques discussed will help you do just that.

Where direct booking examples are discussed, you will see a small symbol beside them.

Sea Zen as a case study

This book gives more than just a formula. I use our Sea Zen VR as a case study that's rich in examples and stories, even failures, to illustrate the abstract principles.

Key point summaries

At the start of each chapter, there is a succinct bullet summary of the important learning points. You can use them to quickly dive into the chapter to immerse yourself in the ideas and examples—and master the techniques presented.

Action is the key to results

The one thing that is critical above all others is taking action. It is a wonderful exercise to acquire new knowledge like reading this book. But knowledge means nothing unless it is applied. There are several quizzes that give you a reality check on whether you are taking action.

Strap in, hold on and enjoy the ride!

Roadmap To Success

It can be overwhelming trying to do everything at once when you are getting started on your journey to high occupancy for your vacation rental.

Fortunately, I have developed a roadmap that can help you focus on the right things in the right order and ultimately achieve high occupancy. The timescale is in three chunks, for a brand-new vacation rental. If you already have a well-established rental, you can still use the roadmap for a makeover to improve your occupancy.

This roadmap is designed specifically for owners of one to three VRs. For larger VRs, see the end of the chapter.

ROADMAP TO SUCCESS

1–6 months

Grow bookings

Sacrifice prices
Relax rules
Grow 5-star reviews
Professional photos
Fine-tune processes

6–18 months

Consolidate

Restore prices
Insiders guides
Newsletter
Website
Stand out

18+ months

Mastery

Increase occupancy
Newsletter, SEO, Ads, PR, Mastermind
Reduce OTAs

The first six months

The emphasis during this period is to get as many bookings as you can and build your reputation and your foundations for later success. It is hard work. You will not make much money.

The online travel agencies that you initially depend on use positive feedback loops, rewarding successful VRs that have good reviews and high bookings. You need to do what it takes to get swept up inside those positive feedback loops so you get listed high on the OTA websites.

You will need to compromise on margins by **sacrificing your price,** maybe setting it 30% under the market! You will need to **relax your operating rules,** accepting most bookings within reason, even if that means instant booking, accepting late guest cancellations, and avoiding cancellations on your part. You might even accept one-night bookings. Don't worry; you can tighten up your rules later.

You need to be generous to your guests and go out of your way to delight them, because during this stage you want to get as many **5-star reviews** as you can, as quickly as you can. You need to be attentive and energetic in meeting your guests' needs. You encourage them to tell their friends about their experience. You capture their email addresses. You are building the foundations of your loyalty program.

You get **professional photos** done, showcasing your fine-tuned VR.

You also **fine-tune your processes** to make your work more efficient, as outlined in chapters 8 to 16. The booking confirmation process is slick and efficient. You develop Q&As for your guests. Your cleaner knows exactly how your VR is to be presented every time and has clear online information about upcoming bookings. Everything runs like clockwork.

This is also the time you need to be listening to your guests' reactions to your VR. See Chapter 19: Customer Feedback Obsession and Chapter 21: Stand Out With A Theme. What do they like?

What is missing? You quickly respond to their reactions and fine-tune your offering. You also modify your description in your listings to mirror your guests' positive comments. You can also experiment with a theme that differentiates you from your competitors. Most VR owners fail to do this.

It is a time when you are working hard building a solid foundation for the future.

Six to 18 months

This is a period of consolidation. Assuming your initial efforts have been successful, and you have a good track record of bookings and 5-star reviews, the online travel agencies will now be ranking you higher on their lists and the bookings will keep coming.

With steady incoming bookings and a solid review reputation, you can quietly **restore your prices** closer to the market rate. You can tighten up your house rules to stricter cancellation policies. You may want to make the minimum stay period longer and no longer accept one-night bookings.

You develop extra information for your guests—your **insider's guides**, including advice on places to eat and attractions in the areas. You promote them on your online travel agency listings.

Though you only have a small number of past guests, you can start your **newsletter** to past guests offering them interesting news snippets and discounts.

The time you spent earlier fussing over guests to get 5-star reviews can now be reallocated to more advanced activities described in chapters 22 to 30, like your **website** and your loyalty program.

You can set up your website and claim your free Google My Business listing. You can set up your online booking calendar so you can take direct bookings easily.

You can experiment with a theme that helps you **stand out** from your competitors, that will surprise and delight your guests and motivate them to tell their friends.

Beyond 18 months

You continue pushing up your prices to the sweet spot where your guests are happy to pay extra for a premium product, without compromising on the volume of bookings, so your occupancy stays high. This takes some experimenting and a careful eye on what your competition is doing.

You fine-tune your tactics for **growing occupancy**—chapters 31 to 43.

During this time your loyalty program is bedding in. Your list of past guests is steadily growing. Your **newsletters are regular**, and you are getting feedback from past guests on how frequently they like getting them. Past guests often re-book after getting the newsletter.

You are posting helpful local information to your website that will be found on Google for specific local searches to help your **SEO** and get more direct bookings.

You can start to experiment with more advanced techniques shown in chapters 44–51. You can set up your own **mastermind group** with other advanced owners. You can see if there are any useful social media channels that are working for others. You can experiment—cautiously—with **Google Ads and Facebook ads**. You can seek out **publicity** from travel journalists.

Over time, as your list of loyal past guests grows, your direct bookings and your occupancy grow. In time, you can cut back on your reliance on the online travel agencies. You are reaching mastery!

Extra—roadmap for larger-scale vacation rentals

The roadmap above is for small VRs of one to three properties. For larger-scale rentals the roadmap is similar, but larger operations must focus much more on automation and standardization.

While a small operator can have simple manual systems like a spreadsheet, a larger operator must have totally standardized pro-cesses that can be used by multiple staff. Larger operations also need a good software package to automate taking bookings and managing all the VR processes.

For small operators, the guest relationship is personal. For large operators the guest relationship becomes one of efficiency, reliability, and high standards, where any one of several staff may assist the guest, and the result will always be a high-quality experience.

For smaller operators, the newsletter is personal and based on a relationship. This is much harder for large operations where there are multiple staff contact points and rarely a tight relationship. For that reason, newsletters are less effective for larger operations.

For larger operations, efficiencies of scale mean that there are more resources to put into the website and marketing. Scale allows extra resources for online marketing, SEO, and paid advertising. As larger VR operations grow, their business may morph into a property management company that manages other owners' vacation rentals.

If you want to keep growing into a larger operation, all credit to you; there are many successful property management companies out there doing very well. That type of operation is beyond the scope of this book.

• • •

You must be clear about your goals. Mine have always been to stay small and achieve outstanding results with close ties to my guests, giving them exceptional experiences. It brings happiness to many people. It is one of the most rewarding lifestyles that anyone can have.

This book is about staying small and performing exceptionally well. It is the road to mastery.

> **Key takeaway: the roadmap is a handy guide to what you should concentrate on as you start your rental.**

Mindset

"Whether you think you can, or you think you can't—you're right."
Henry Ford

The main factor in achieving vacation rental results is your attitude.

Ours is a wonderful industry where you can build your own small business in your own style as fast or slow as your own actions determine. Determination, curiosity, creativity, and self-belief are critical. There are easy things to do, and lots of challenges. For each challenge, you need to summon the courage to attack and master it.

Vacation rental mindset

Several years ago, two different VR owners asked me to coach them to improve their vacation rentals.

One, called Danka, eagerly absorbed everything I showed her. Within a month she was using the new methods, and within three months she was well booked. She kept coming back with new questions and acted on the answers. When she found barriers, she found ways around them. When the online travel agencies caused her problems with glitches in their systems, she found a rep and challenged them. She had close conversations with the guests who stayed in her VR, and they often re-booked the next year.

Within nine months she had started a second rental, and it too was successful. If she met a challenge she went off and found ways to fix it.

In contrast, the other person, called Mary, was exposed to the same information but took an entirely different approach, deeply in avoidance. "Um, I've been busy this week" and "I just don't feel right calling my guests after they email me …" If there was an opportunity, she was reluctant to seize it. A year later, little had changed in her business.

The two people were exposed to the same information, but different mindsets led to different outcomes.

It can be daunting with so much to do in the early days of running a VR, but just pressing forward a step at a time is all it takes.

My suggested approach is:

- Get your basics done with smallest distraction possible.
- Decide the few big things that will give you the most impact— this book is designed to help you understand what those few big things are.
- Work on the first of those big things a step at a time: try it, test, modify, and bolt down into a standard system that works for you.

- If you strike a barrier, be creative or ask for advice and persist. Remember, barriers are great. Once you've got through them, you are a good step ahead of your competitors.
- Just keep going.

PART 2

BASICS FOR HIGH OCCUPANCY

So you have your vacation rental set up. Maybe you have been operating for years or maybe you are starting for the first time. What are the vital few things you need to do to be successful?

Don't skip over the basics. Many who have been in the business for years and feel destined for low rentals often have not got their foundation right. This is so important, but so many get it wrong. Unless you have these foundations right, you will fail to reach your potential.

Using this part of the book, you can step through your own basics and get them right as a firm foundation for improving the guest experience and your own higher occupancy.

CHAPTER 8

Best Website Listings

KEY POINTS

- The best sites to list on can be very different between locations and types of accommodation.
- Simple Google searches usually uncover the best places to list.
- Simply checking with the experience of your local network can confirm the best sites.
- Missing good sites can be very costly in terms of lost bookings.

In the disrupted world of internet sales, your property must be listed in the places your customers are looking, the best-performing websites. These will usually be one of the large online travel agency listing sites like HomeAway or Airbnb, but not always.

The best site will be unique to your area and your customers, not a universal answer.

Five years ago, I was amused by a question on a global VR forum, where a VR owner in Portugal asked, "Where is the best place to list my villa?" In a crazy thread, well-meaning owners from all over the world gave their advice, with a long stream of suggestions based on successes in their own locations—all worthless, because he asked the wrong question of the wrong people.

What VR owners need to ask is, "Where are *my* target customers searching and what do they find at the top?"

Using the 80/20 principle, a few Google searches will find the obvious solution.

> Keywords → Google search → Top listing sites

In most cases, the customer will start by searching Google for the keywords of **location** and **type of accommodation**.

This is best shown by an example.

In a town near me called Lorne, most customers wanting to go on holiday search Google using the keywords "lorne accommodation." Typically, the results they get are for Wotif, HomeAway and TripAdvisor, with ads from Booking.com, Wotif and Airbnb, all global corporations.

> "lorne accommodation" → Google search → Wotif, HomeAway, TripAdvisor, Booking.com, Airbnb

So, in our example, should an owner in Lorne list on Wotif? Not necessarily.

The first search should be followed up by other searches. In the Lorne holiday house market, customers are looking for holiday houses for a holiday, so a smart owner would also search for "lorne holiday house" and "lorne holiday" and "lorne getaway." In a few years the market may shift to other sites. The idea is to follow the market changes and be on the most relevant sites.

In other locales the principle is the same, but the keywords and the best site to list on will vary. For example, in the US, someone looking for a vacation in San Diego searching for "san diego vacation" or "san diego accommodation" will find TripAdvisor, FlipKey, Expedia and Wotif. In that market, FlipKey might be an obvious place to list.

So what are *your* keywords?

If you are not sure of the keywords for your customers for your area, ask the authority—your customer. Obviously, this works best after you are established, but it is very powerful. You have the customer on the phone while they are inquiring or booking, so just say, "And one last thing, how did you find us? Do you remember what you started searching for?" Most folks have a very good idea and will tell you.

The power of brand

Sometimes, when asked how they search, folks will just say, "I always use Booking.com"—or HomeAway, or VRBO, or Airbnb, etc. Take note carefully and stay alert for emerging trends. Some sites are brilliant at creating brand awareness, like Airbnb. Your customers don't always start with a general search; in fact, some start at their favorite listing site. If that's the case, tune into your customers and go where they go!

Ask your network

Another way of choosing the best place to list is to network with other VR owners nearby. Often fellow owners are technically competitors but are amazingly helpful in sharing information. VR owners usually have a common competitor in hotels so will see other VR owners as colleagues. "My competitor's competitor is my friend."

The choice of main listing site is very important, so take the time to make those simple Google searches and ensure you are listed where your customers are searching.

In the turbulent world of VR rentals, the results are constantly shifting. You should check Google for your keywords every six months to see if there are any shifts.

The shotgun method

If you can't check with colleagues and you find the Google analysis above daunting, you can just try the likely candidates and see what works. You might just blast away like a shotgun that scatters enough over the target to get results. List on five or six sites and see what happens and which works best for you. Be careful to not list on too many. To list on multiple sites, you need to be organized to minimize work. You should have:

- your pics, text and rates in one place to make listing easy
- a spreadsheet of usernames and passwords
- notes on how to update each calendar and make bookings
- an understanding of how to rank high on each site. Decide whether you want to pay the fee or devote the time to ride the algorithm to the top. This is not trivial!

For some owners this becomes a treadmill, demanding to operate and confusing to evaluate. I once met an owner who had listed on 23 sites and was overwhelmed and exhausted. Worse, she hadn't pruned to the vital few sites and was even performing badly on them due to lack of attention.

If you do use the shotgun method and try all the likely suspects, take time to analyze the results after a few months, then keep the winners and kill the others! In most cases, owners could have found the answers in an hour of analysis or a few phone calls to colleagues.

I prefer to check the obvious on Google for my keywords as described above, and to share wisdom with colleagues to cut short the huge effort of multiple sites.

> In most cases, owners could have found the best places to list in an hour of analysis or a few phone calls

Where not to list

The advice I give you here is gold: do not try to list on every website out there and certainly not on every one that knocks on your door.

VR owners will find a constant stream of new entrants into the listing market, each pitching offers to the unsuspecting owner. "We are the fastest growing website for your market, get in now with our free offer and reap the rewards …" When you get these offers, just go back to Google with your target keywords and see how this new market entrant is faring in the real world of search results. Unless they are in the top few results, ignore them, and maybe check six months later to see if the promises have eventuated.

A "free" listing is never really free. It takes time, energy and focus in getting started and maintaining your listing and calendar. Your focus needs to be on the main game of keeping loyal guests.

Advanced tip on listing sites

Later in this book you will find a paradox. I will be showing you how to become less dependent on listing sites. The more successful you are, the greater your ability to bring guests to your rental without using a listing site. However, take one step at a time. In the beginning, you really *need* these listing sites.

YOU CAN LEAD A HORSE TO WATER ...

Some years ago, a friend asked what I thought of several different listing sites for his rentals. I gave him my thoughts on which were the best and why. I even gave him a tip on how the algorithm worked so he could list high easily. He thanked me but said he thought the commission was too high, so kept to his favorite sites.

Over the years, I estimate that that decision cost him A$70,000 per year, even after taking the commission into account. The wrong decision on choosing listing sites can be very costly. It's worth taking the time to get it right.

Key takeaway: use Google and your network to verify the best sites to list on.

CHAPTER 9

Excellent Photographs

KEY POINTS

- Your key, or hero, shot is the most important factor in people booking your VR.
- Your hero shot should be taken by a professional photographer.
- Take care to plan for and attend the photo shoot.
- Studies show a target of 20–30 photos is okay.
- Take two to three photos of most rooms and one of the main appliances.
- A floor plan and 360-degree video will improve bookings.

You need excellent photographs. A picture really does tell a thousand words.

Okay, you might think everyone knows that. No, you need really, really good photographs. This is not negotiable if you are serious about getting bookings. Photographs are the way you establish trust, answer questions, realize dreams for your guests and ultimately make the sale.

Before you skip to the next topic, read this story about how understanding photographs gave the Airbnb founders another step up on the path to market domination.

HOW BETTER PHOTOGRAPHS SAVED AIRBNB:

In the early years of Airbnb, the founders polished their model, but for some reason it was not quite working, even in the important market of New York, where they got most bookings. So they went to New York with the burning question of why and what they could do about it.

They visited as many listing owners as they could. They soon found that the photographs posted by most owners didn't do justice to the great selling features of each listing. So they took their own good photographs and changed the photos on the listings.

Then they discovered something astounding. The number of bookings doubled, and slowly the company grew to success.

A photograph was not just nice to have; it was fundamental to their future success. It is no accident that in its growth stage Airbnb offered free photographs to owners.

Airbnb has become far more sophisticated in recent years, conducting many experiments about how renters respond to different photographs. I spoke with their global gurus at the Airbnb Open in Paris in 2015, and this is what they found:

- The main shot is crucial. It should be taken by a professional.
- Each room should have two to three shots so a renter can totally trust what they are seeing is what they will get. You are creating trust.
- Go easy on wide-angle shots that make a place look bigger than it really is. You are creating trust.
- Take a pic of every featured appliance like TVs, washers, driers, etc. Many renters will skim over lists and forget about features but will vividly recall an image of the appliance. This will help you stand out above other offers.
- It's not too many to have 20–30 photos.

I used to wonder if it was important for my properties, until I started asking guests why they booked with me. About half of them said, "I just really like the look of your place in the photos." One even said, "The photo just called out to me, I just have to go there!"

The critical learning here is **get a professional to shoot your key photos.** Here are some of the reasons why good photography is hard.

The classic problem of an external view

A high proportion of VRs will have a hero shot looking from a gorgeous room out to a gorgeous view. It turns out that this is a problem to photograph.

Have you ever looked at rental photographs of a view that didn't work? It's common to see a gorgeous view and a gloomy room, or a bright room and total whiteness outside.

This is because cameras can't accurately sense the huge variation that the human eye can. In a room with a view, our eyes adjust to see the bright outside view and the details inside the room. However, a camera can't (yet) do this adjustment automatically. It can see the bright view *or* the inside detail of the room, but not both.

The HDR solution

HDR stands for high dynamic range imaging, which gives a perfect shot in severely contrasting light. The skilled HDR photographer takes about three shots with different brightness settings, and software stitches them together for a perfect result. The inside of the room is vibrant *and* the external view pops. It is usually done on the spot with a laptop to check that the result works well. It's easy for the professional; they do it well.

Another solution is to try to match the inside and outside light. This can be done by adding lights inside or by waiting till just the right moment when inside and outside light is matching, like at dusk. It is tricky to get everything right, whereas a professional with HDR will get it right for most of the bright day.

Can you do it yourself? Sure. But how do you want to spend your time? Should you spend your time training to become an amateur photographer or get the pro to do the photos while you do the hard yards in smart marketing that gives you more bookings? I suggest the latter.

The one time when DIY photos are okay

There is one time when it's okay to take your own amateur photos, and that is right at the start when you're setting up your rental for the first time. You are starting to put everything in place, but nothing is settled. It's all a fluid process. You are arranging furniture, trying decorations, settling into a theme, trying bed dressing, and swapping things around. Maybe you're still waiting on that special table or outdoor furniture.

You need some photos to put on listing sites to get started, knowing you still haven't got the finished article. Don't delay the marketing. Just take some reasonable photos yourself and get the marketing underway.

But this doesn't get you off the hook from getting some fabulous professional photos. Schedule the professional shoot when the dust has settled and you have that "finished" look. You can easily upload the photos onto the marketing websites any time.

Preparing for the professional shoot

Your preparation work starts long before the shoot.

1. **You should have your theme clear.** How will you show yourself so you stand out from your competitors? Do your homework and see what competitors have done and make yourself different. What will your hero or money shot look like, the one featured large on the websites? If competitors all have similar living rooms looking out to the same view, make yours different.
2. **Declutter.** No wires, no strings, minimum gadgets on the benches. Everything clean, so the eye will go to your best features.

3. **Create some interest and color.** Have you seen those images of a room with gray furniture on gray floor looking out to a gray-blue sky? Boring! Make sure there is some life in the room, some red or yellow cushions. Choose your   wall pictures with the photographs in mind.

4. **Think about your guest experience.** If your guests will sit outside with a glass of wine and some flowers on the table, then plan to arrange to set up the table, and have some red napkins for color.

5. **Warmth.** Is there a fireplace? Arrange for a blaze on the day. The photographer can take a shot of the fire at its best and if it has died out by the time of the final shot, the photographer can Photoshop it back in later.

6. **Keep it real.** What you show in the photographs is what your guests should see when they arrive. There are amazing stories of owners bringing the good furniture from home for the shoot and replacing it later with cheap alternatives. Nothing more likely to disappoint guests and trigger a dispute, just dumb!

7. **Check out your photographer beforehand.** What is their work like? Discuss the impression you are looking for and the best time of day for the shoot when the light will be best for your rental. Be clear that you will own the photographs and that you get a full set of large file size final images, typically 3MB or more in jpg format. How long will it take for them to do final adjustments? Be clear on the number of photographs you are you expecting, and of course the price.

8. **Scope.** The photographer will need to get a feel for the number of rooms to be covered. As a minimum you will need several bedrooms, living, kitchen, bathroom, good aspects of the view if you have one, the exterior, and any special features like spa, pool, fireplace, entertaining, garden. And don't forget your theme. In my different rentals over the years, it has included treetop views, pets, wild birds, Indigenous art, the beach, urban chic, Japanese

styling, romance, and more as I experimented with different themes and ideas. Not all at once and not all in the same rental of course.

9. Remember too **you will need quite a few good shots**. Many of the online listing companies have found that listings need more than 20 images, and even 30 is okay. They have found that those with 20 images perform better than those with 10!

You may need to take a few extra photos yourself of the local attractions the beach the shops, the tourist icons, so guests can get a feel of what there is to do in the area. They don't have to be the same high quality as your rental.

Shooting on the day

1. Get your preparation and decluttering done early. Be present at the shoot and work with the photographer. Some owners go off on more important errands and complain later about the choice of photographs. **You need to be there.**

2. Remind the photographer of your requirements but be prepared to listen and **give them freedom to use their skills** to help show off your rental's best features.

3. Ask that they **go easy on the wide-angle shots**. Using a very wide angle can make a small room look huge, but explain that there's no point if you are going to have disappointed guests later.

4. **Go easy on the fluffy close-ups** of the smart coffee cups. While they can convey atmosphere, your guests really need to know what the rooms look like.

5. Then **let them get on with it**. They will be thinking about perspectives, the light, lenses, and more. You are there in the background to answer questions if needed.

6. If you are trying to get a shot of a fabulous view, **sunlight can be important,** and the photographer may need to come back. My photographer once came on the only foggy day all year, so the

view was nil. He took all the other shots, and I negotiated that he would drop by a week later on another job to take that one photograph—and it was worth it.

Why bother with all this? You need to stand out! Photography is one of the most important investments you can make. Good photographs will return the investment many times over.

Getting professional photographs for free

Airbnb still believes in the power of good photographs. While in the early years they arranged photographs for free, now you can "request a quote" through the Airbnb system. See www.airbnb. com.au/professional_photography.

Some enterprising VR owners contact professional photographers and offer free accommodation in return for professional photos. It is a bit hit and miss, depending on finding a deal that suits both parties.

Floor plan

A good floor plan as part of your images helps your guests understand your facilities, and helps you get more bookings. You can make one yourself on PowerPoint, or pay someone else to prepare one, e.g. Fiverr.com.

360 video

Again, a good video walkthrough will help your prospective guests understand and trust your VR and get you more bookings. You can do it yourself with a smartphone and upload the video to YouTube. You can then edit it, adding a title, URL, or even music, using the free YouTube video editor. (Search "how to use the youtube video editor.")

Or you can use a commercial provider to make a proper 360 video that works interactively to allow you to look around the room. (Search "360 video.")

Once on YouTube, the video can be embedded on your own website. Your video on YouTube should have your URL for direct bookings.

You can also upload your video to the online travel agencies, but it should have no URL, or they will reject it.

I've made several videos on a smartphone—a little fiddly, but they work well. If you have a few hours, it can be fun, and you can achieve amazing results. A professional provider will cost more but will do all the hard work and uploading for you.

> **Key takeaway: use a professional photographer to take your hero shot.**

CHAPTER 10

Accurate Calendar And Pricing

KEY POINTS

- Keep calendars and pricing accurate at all times to maximize bookings and reduce ranking penalties.
- Carefully decide whether to allow instant bookings— several factors apply.
- Shortcuts can help you manually update four calendars in under three minutes—suitable for one to three VRs.
- Channel managers are cost-effective for updating calendars for large numbers of VRs.

Booking a holiday rental is about trust; the guests should be confident in what they are going to get with your rental.

Uncertainty about price and availability is a real turnoff for prospective guests as they browse for their holiday. Is the rental available for their dates? What is the real price? Are there any hidden extras? Am I wasting my time and energy inquiring about something that is not available or too expensive?

The big listing sites know all this, and some provide incentives or penalties to encourage accuracy of calendars and pricing. Booking.com will instantly book available dates in the owner's calendar, and if you are already booked you have to pay to relocate the guest's new booking. Similarly, Airbnb has an instant book option and if you cancel that booking, your ranking is penalized, even if you made a slip in pricing or availability.

> I had a friend once in the industry who deliberately kept her calendar showing mostly "available" when in fact she was already booked. She said, "I like to be in control, and if I'm booked for the dates they are inquiring about, I try to convince them to change their plans to another date when I'm free."
>
> She wasted a lot of time and effort, and ultimately had fewer bookings than for accurate calendars.

The benefits of accuracy are considerable:

- The inquirer has confidence that it's worth inquiring, you get more well-qualified inquiries and bookings, and the ease of making an inquiry enhances your brand and increases the chance of repeat business.
- With calendars up-to-date, you can allow "instant booking" on some websites, which attracts more inquiries and more bookings.

> The best approach is to be organized with prices and dates and have them 100% accurate all the time

So there are good reasons *why* you should be accurate, but *how* do you do it if you are listed on three, four or more listing sites?

How to easily manage calendars

It's about getting organized and having a system.

Once you are organized, you can update your calendars as you take a booking, in less than a minute per calendar. So if you are listed on four listing sites and you have four calendars to update, it takes just three minutes to update them all on a laptop—not such a challenge. I've done it thousands of times. It's not possible to do it on smartphones in my experience, but this may change.

The first step is to bookmark the calendar page of each listing site and get your browser to remember the username and password. This is a standard feature in Chrome and Firefox.

Then you group these bookmarks in a folder in your browser and open them all together (right click, open all). Voila—within a few seconds you have four calendars open, and you can amend each calendar. In a few minutes it's all done.

> You can manually update four calendars in under three minutes!

Instant book problems

If you have several online travel agencies using instant book like Airbnb and Booking.com, there is a risk of an automated double booking, e.g. while you are asleep.

However, the risk is very, very small (it has never happened to me), and there are ways of minimizing damage.

Airbnb will remove superhost status for unwarranted cancelled bookings, but it does allow a cancellation without penalty if you are **uncomfortable with the reservation.** (Rules apply.) Booking.com allows cancellation if the guest's card doesn't work or they ask you to arrange a new booking for a double-booked guest at your cost. The world won't end!

If you are uncomfortable with the very small risk, don't turn on instant book or avoid using Booking.com.

The power of scripts

If you find the different calendars confusing, you can write down a "script," with screenshots. This is just a simple cheat sheet showing the steps you can use to jog your memory on how each calendar works. After you've done it a few times, it becomes automatic.

Keeping pricing accurate

Again, it's about getting organized. Keep a simple file that documents your decisions that you can refer to later.

Start with the periods of the year where rates change, such as public holidays and peak holiday season. It pays to do this a few years ahead so it's all in one place.

In my holiday area, I have a standard weekend and midweek rate, then different rates for the five-week peak summer season and others for holiday weekends. It is all documented in one place, including any variations between listing sites and my own sites.

Armed with your blueprint, you can systematically load your prices into your various listing websites. This will take a while, as each listing site has its own pricing formulas and updating systems. Periodically, you should revisit your pricing and adjust it. Pricing strategies are a whole different subject that takes into account your occupancy, your competitors, and any new events that emerge.

Automatic pricing

Several of the online travel agencies have automatic pricing suggestions; however, I've found they are for average VRs with average market rates. For readers of this book who are offering a premium-priced VR, automated pricing systems will undercut your margins, so don't use them unless you understand the implications.

Channel managers

I think I've heard across the ether someone calling out to me, "You've forgotten the channel managers!"

A channel manager is a wonderful piece of software—in theory. It is a master calendar linking to all your listing sites, and when you take a booking, you just update the channel manager master, and the dates are instantly updated across all the calendars across all your listing sites. Similarly, if you change a price in one location, the price is replicated across all your listing sites. See Chapter 50: Channel Managers.

The only problem is that at the time of writing (2018), some of the listing sites that we in the vacation rental industry use lack an interface to the channel managers or have a delayed synch cycle. So you have some *extra* channel manager software that you need to control that still doesn't do the entire job. And some of these channel managers come with hefty fees and commissions.

Channel managers are great for hotels, motels, multi-unit condominiums, and the like. Lots of similar units under one ownership can be listed on hundreds of listing sites. However, currently channel managers don't seem to include all the sites the VR owners would like to use, including local or regional listing sites.

Maybe one day there will be a channel manager that interfaces to all the listing sites that a VR owner might want—speed the day! For now, manual updating methods work well for VR owners who just own one or a few properties.

> Key takeaway: keep calendars and prices up-to-date; manual updating is okay.

CHAPTER 11

A Name That Stands Out

> **KEY POINTS**
> - Your VR name is a way to reinforce your presence across multiple websites.
> - It helps guests book direct when you have your own website.
> - Online travel agencies want to hide your brand and reinforce their own.
> - There are eight guidelines for choosing a name.

You need to plan ahead and early on choose a distinctive name for your VR.

It is the name inquirers will see on multiple listing sites and your own website. It is the name past guests will remember and search for. It is the name friends of past guests will look for when referred by your guests, and it is the name your own friends and family will look for.

It's the way that guests will find you and book direct later when you have your own website. No matter if you don't have a website just now; they are getting simpler, easier, and cheaper. The main thing is to reinforce your brand everywhere until you do have your own website.

It's a bonus if the name is evocative of the experience, e.g. "Ocean Blue." The main point is to be memorable.

There is a great game going on at a high level with titles and descriptions that you need to be aware of here. You need to understand the game.

The big listing sites want to own your listing as a confusing commodity so inquirers can't find you elsewhere. They don't want you to establish your brand. That's why the likes of Airbnb encourage unsuspecting owners to create descriptive listing titles in 35 characters like "Stylish 2BR with amazing sea views." Any returning guests will remember the parent brand, Airbnb, not the confusing "Stylish 2BR with amazing sea views." The only way returning guests will find you is via the parent brand, if you are lucky.

"Ocean Blue with amazing sea views" is evocative and memorable.

So this is the great game:
On the one hand, you want to establish your rental name as a brand for loyalty. On the other hand, the mega listing companies want to obliterate your name and reinforce their own brand.

Choosing a name

Your name should be memorable, evocative, and interesting, if possible. My wife and I created Treetops Wye River and Sea Zen as memorable names that start to tell a story and create some interest. Often a noun and a color are memorable, like "Ocean Blue" above, or "Red Door."

A secondary feature is getting a name close to *a* in the alphabet. While the mega listing sites will rank rental listings by factors like reviews, conversions, etc., a surprising number of smaller sites will list properties alphabetically. Smartphones list names alphabetically too.

When we were setting up our holiday rental in the Melbourne suburb of Richmond, Sibylle and I spent a full day (really!) brainstorming an evocative name. We finally settled on "Alto Richmond." It was memorable, high in the alphabet, and as it means "high" in the romance languages, it was appropriate for a place located in our area of Richmond Hill.

It was simple, memorable, just two syllables, and it resonated with the "hill" theme. It also didn't conflict with competitors, and although the domain name Alto.com. au was *not* available, we registered Altorichmond.com.au, which helped our return guests find our website.

If all else fails, you can use the street name. "14 Broad St, chic townhouse" is far better than "2-bedroom chic comfy townhouse." The street name can also help inquirers find which part of town it's in.

Your brand name

The choice of name is not trivial. In summary, it should have as many of the following attributes as possible:

- related to your theme where relevant
- memorable
- one or two syllables
- unique to your area
- suitable for a website name—is a domain name available?
- easily pinpointed in a Google search
- not trademarked by someone else who will sue you!
- preferably closer to *a* than *z* (some lists are still ranked alphabetically).

The battle for memories

Yes, you are in a battle for people's memories. The online travel agencies want you to confuse your past guests and only recall the OTA name. You want to use your brand name at every opportunity.

As well as the title, you can also weave it into the first paragraph of description. "At Ocean Blue, a sparkling new house overlooking the sea, you can let your worries float away ..." and so on.

So, you use your creativity to emphasize your name in the OTA listings.

You also use your creativity with your guests to emphasize your name with them at every contact:

- "Thank you for booking Red Door ..."
- "Getting access to Red Door is easy ..."
- "If you have any issues while staying at Red Door, just call me ..."
- "The Red Door information folder ..."
- "Thank you for staying at Red Door ..."
- "Red Door discount for past guests and their friends ..."
- "We hope you can help us by leaving a review for Red Door ..."

Your name is important. It's the way that smart searchers **will find you to book direct.** That in turn will bring you more bookings and higher margins.

Key takeaway: using your VR name consistently can help get direct bookings.

CHAPTER 12

A Description That Stands Out

KEY POINTS

- Use your title and description to stand out from your competitors and get more bookings.
- Capture compliments from your guests and use that language in your descriptions.
- Use your VR name in your listing title to maximize your chances of separate direct bookings.

So you are thinking about your listing—existing or proposed—on your target websites.

You need a description will achieve these six things:

1. Stand out and get noticed.
2. Speak to your target customers.
3. Exploit your theme and image.
4. Use the emotional language of your customers.
5. Give the facts in your description.
6. Use a title that works for you.

Sameness is death! Difference is safe!

1. Stand out and get noticed

A very cool fact about the vacation rental industry is that our guests choose our properties because we are different. If they wanted a standard experience, they would have chosen a hotel, where everything is predictable.

In the same way, they will be looking for something different when they look through the long list of properties offered on the listing pages. If you are one of 20 similar-looking places with similar descriptions such as "Comfortable house with great view", then you are saying just roll the dice and maybe choose me.

But if you are different, the inquirer will look past the 20 similar places and check you out. Your image title and description need to stand out. But how?

2. Speak to your target customers

You want to stand out, but to whom? Your target customers.

Who are they? Are they families? Romantic couples? Golfers? Food lovers? Fishing enthusiasts? Lovers of chic modern houses? Lovers of rustic houses?

Think about your area, the strengths of your property, your interests, the people who already come to the area. In our three-bedroom coastal house in the rainforest, my target market was families with dogs. In our one-bedroom studio at the beach, my target market is couples who want a luxury experience. In our three-bedroom city house, my target market was visiting interstate families. In a friend's suburban house with four bedrooms and two living areas, it is large interstate groups.

You don't need to be too hung up on this, and your market may shift over time with experience, but initially you should have a fairly clear target customer. Targeting everyone is targeting no one. Pick your target market and move on.

3. Exploit your theme and image

Theme? What theme, you say?

When styling your rental, you have the opportunity to create a look and feel that is interesting and plays to your strengths. You should also play to your target market. When writing your description, you can exploit those to stand out.

You can have some fun with your theme. If you are targeting surfing enthusiasts, you might have a surfboard on the ceiling and some pictures of the classic surfing heroes. Your shelves will include some surfing books, and you might have an in-house guide to the best surfing spots and the best surf shop.

If you are targeting bird lovers, have pictures of birds on the walls, bird books available, and some binoculars handy. You might have tips on local birds and how to find them. If you are targeting food enthusiasts, you might set up the kitchen so guests can cook up a storm and include food pictures and books and videos.

You don't have to overdo it, but you can create a point of difference. You can play on your theme in your hero image to stand out. You can play on your theme with a description that stands out.

When my wife and I purpose-built the rental studio beside our house, our target market was romantic couples on a luxury getaway. We had an interest in Japanese design and chose Japanese Zen as our theme.

We included Japanese shoji screens, some prints, fabrics, and crockery from Japan, and some related books. The name "Sea Zen" hints at something relaxing by the sea, with a Japanese flavor. I have lots to talk about in our description.

There is a lot more on themes in the advanced part of this book in Chapter 21: Standing Out With A Theme.

4. Use the emotional language of your customers

When an inquirer is searching for a vacation rental, deep down they are searching for an emotional experience. It may be a feeling of relaxing, learning, excitement, adventure, reflection, family times, intimacy, bonding, and more. **You can tap into the guests' deep psychological needs.**

When you write your description with words that match the inquirer's emotional mood, the inquirer notices your offer. You are answering a need that they may not have even consciously known, and you are on the way to connecting, and then an inquiry, and then a booking. You are using psychology to help get the booking.

But how do you know what your target guests are looking for?

> **Your guests tell you what they are looking for**

Chances are your guests are already telling you, and in the most detailed language possible, exactly what they are looking for.

After you have been operating for a while, you will be building up comments in your guest book (yes, you should have a guest book in your VR!) and reviews on your listing site. You have a written catalog of the way folks are thinking about your rental. You have a catalog of the emotional phrases you can use in your description.

You should also be talking—at least some of the time—to your guests after their stay to ask them how it went. This can be face to face or by telephone. The replies can be vague, but sometimes guests are floating on air as they depart after a fabulous emotional experience.

If you are alert to this, their comments will be very detailed, with amazing insights. This tells you what is resonating deeply with their inner needs. Then all you have to do is write it down for others with similar needs. When they see the words, they will think, "That is exactly what I am looking for!"

When they make a deep emotional connection, minor details like price become irrelevant. When they book with you, they will say something like "It is exactly what we are looking for" or "We just can't wait to come, we are so excited." As an owner, with no exaggeration, I have lost count of the times that guests have said exactly those words.

5. Give the facts in your description

Your inquirers will need to know the basics: capacity, beds, bathrooms, kitchen, view, fire, pet policy.

Include the number of people your rental sleeps, the number of beds and the type/size. Most listing sites will have capacity and beds listed superficially, but you can flesh out the detail. If the beds have views, let the inquirers know. If they split apart for flexibility, or for bunks, tell them. If beds are made up with fresh linen and towels are included, tell them. If beds are comfortable, let them know, as this is a big deal for many guests.

All these details should be included somewhere, but not right at the top. Start describing the experience first. You can do this based on how you would feel about staying there. Later, when you accumulate a lot of reviews, you will find some that describe their experience so evocatively that you can use their words in your description. It will call out to searching guests and resonate with the very experiences that the searching guests are looking for.

> **How evocative guest comments can guide your description**
>
> "We had the most relaxed time at Sea Zen. It was absolutely heavenly. Zen is the most apt description. As far as I'm concerned, they have thought of absolutely everything. A truly beautiful, outstanding place to dream, create, live & simply be."

"A beautiful retreat in a perfect location! The Zen-inspired apartment is very relaxing, and the spa and the steam shower was a great way to unwind from a busy lifestyle. We fell in love with the beach, the local wildlife, the walks and the pub, all in close proximity. It was a great place for a romantic getaway and we would love to visit again soon."

With these words of inspiration, you can make a very appealing description:

"The Zen-inspired apartment is very relaxing, and the spa and the steam shower are a great way to unwind from a busy lifestyle. Fall in love with the beach, the local wildlife. A truly beautiful, outstand0ing place to dream, create, live, and simply be."

6. Use a title that works for you

Your online travel agency title is very important to getting inquiries, as it has quite a few functions.

First and foremost, it should contain your rental name—your brand—to help get direct bookings. As the copywriters say, the photo and title get readers to view the first sentence of the description. The first sentence evokes interest in the second paragraph, and so on to the end.

Some examples of titles

Airbnb gives you just 35 characters for your title. Here is an example of two different titles for the same property, one evocative, one boring.

Treetops—wake to great sea views	3 BR house with great ocean views

I prefer the one on the left. It has the evocative brand name in the title and hints at the experience when you wake in the morning. The one on the right says this is just another three-bedroom house with views. Often the online travel agency will already tell you how many bedrooms there are anyway.

Armed with the brand name, savvy guests can search for your website and book direct, with savings for the guest and the owner.

> Key takeaway: use your VR name in your listing title to maximize your chances of direct bookings.

CHAPTER 13

A Seamless Cleaning Process

KEY POINTS
- Your VR is a cleaning business first and a marketing business second.
- You cleaner/housekeeper is your partner who will help you achieve outstanding presentation—better than competitors.
- Clean your VR yourself twice a year to keep aware of the challenges.

"It's a cleaning business"

Early in my rental experience with Treetops, a very wise rental manager who had won countless tourism awards told me that, "The holiday rental business is a cleaning business." I was shocked at the time, as I had spent the previous two weeks immersed in ways of improving my internet marketing, totally blind to cleaning.

When you think about it, no matter how good your marketing, the owner needs a way of arranging the cleaning of a rental in the short period between the prior guest checkout and the next guest check-in, even if they're on the same day. It needs to be able to operate flawlessly three or four times a week. It should satisfy these basics:

- The cleaning needs to be thorough, and the standard of presentation needs to be high, if guests are to come back or tell their friends.
- There also needs to be a system for laundering and changing linen, adding soaps and consumables.
- There needs to be a way of handling the times when things go wrong. Problems need to be managed/escalated or reported to the owner.
- Finally, the cleaner needs to know exactly when the clean is to take place, the number of guests, and any special requirements. Ideally, they should download this online.

All these basic processes need to take place seamlessly.

The smart owner will quickly learn that the cleaner is their partner and should be treated with respect. Over time, the relationship can grow where the cleaner develops ownership and pride in the rental and can forestall impending problems.

When you set up your rental, you need to design in your cleaner's needs. A lockable central cleaner's cupboard is essential if you supply any stock.

Some shortsighted owners see the cleaner as an expendable supplier, someone to chisel and hassle to get more output for less payment. That is a very unwise path and a sure way to drop cleaning standards, create poor guest reviews, and generate a whole lot of work in training and induction. How do you want to spend your time as rental owner—retraining disgruntled cleaners or improving your marketing, with cleaning seamless in the background?

For the serious VR owner, it's important to intimately understand the cleaning challenges unique to your property. It is a good idea to stay in your VR yourself as a guest. You also should also clean your entire property yourself, several times, and see the property through the eyes of a cleaner.

> For deep insights into cleaning, clean your property yourself several times

One of my most popular blog posts is "It's a cleaning business," (Brown 2014) in which I talk about my fabulous cleaner Saint Lizzie, who saved me from many a scrape with double bookings and unexpected problems. See it here: www.holidayrentalmastery.com/its-a-cleaning-business.

When you have a good partnership with your cleaner, they will take pride in how your VR performs. They will be happy to call the guest if they are ready early. They will pounce on the guest questionnaire and check the cleaning score. They will let you know the moment they find some property left by departing guests. They will anticipate problems and help you fix them!

Tips:

- Develop a cleaner checklist in consultation with your cleaner, with lots of photos of presentation, and a final checklist for a walkthrough to check key elements.
- Put your schedule of cleaning dates in Google Docs or similar. Your cleaner can download it on their smartphone with one click—easy. This is actually a big deal for keeping your cleaner easily informed.
- The cleaning schedule should list the guest name and mobile so the cleaner can personalize a welcome card and call the guest if ready early.
- Be sure to leave cleaning equipment accessible to guests, so if they want to clean (and many do!), they can clean and save your cleaner valuable time.

Key takeaway: your VR is a cleaning business first and a marketing business second.

CHAPTER 14

The Organized Back Office

You need to have efficient support systems in place.

You are best off in having your own master record-keeping system. Don't use an online travel agency system, which can disappear overnight.

You can use a simple spreadsheet that records customer details, booking details, and payment records. Simple is good. The spreadsheet can be shared with others in the family business using something like Dropbox or Google Drive.

Similarly, you need to keep track of all costs: what is paid to whom for what and when. A simple spreadsheet can work for this too.

The more holiday rentals you manage, the more complicated recording systems become. This book is targeted at owners with one to three rentals. Over about three properties, a commercial backend software system will be worth the cost and effort.

Organizing records

Images and videos need to be kept organized in a system of folders so the originals can be found, along with the sets placed on online travel agency sites.

Master records, spreadsheets, and folders need to be backed up regularly, somewhere like the cloud. Relying on a single PC is a recipe for disaster if it's hacked, stolen, or destroyed.

Payment systems

Somehow you need to get your guests' payments. There are lots of options: bank transfer, credit card, PayPal, and cash. Many listing sites will make a direct deposit into your bank account.

Most guests will expect payment by credit card, and often online. There are benefits in an online credit card payment system that you control, which is what I use. It can be a bother to set up but gives you a lot of flexibility and puts you in control. A merchant facility like your own bank, Stripe, and PayPal are common alternatives.

Documenting your key processes

Take an hour to document the key steps of your most important processes, like taking a booking and updating calendars. Store them away on somewhere like Dropbox, for the times you forget or when you need to train a backup person to keep your business running. Include your key templates, like replies and booking confirmations. Also, securely file your list of passwords—password protected, of course!

If you have the same repeating questions from guests, prepare a Q&A sheet that you can send out or put on your website. There is no point in reinventing the wheel every time you have an inquiry. I have a Q&A page that I send out with my welcome pack to every guest who books. It has saved hundreds of hours over the years.

Be a tech whiz with perfect recall

No one can do that, right? Of course not, but what you can do is keep your own simple tips file with the subject and solution documented. Take a few moments to document and save the key points for each of those tech challenges that crop up from time to time, each of which takes a lot to learn and is easy to forget. I use it for things like a hack to change one online travel agency calendar en masse, an online site to minimize pdf sizes, tips for resizing images, loading to YouTube, etc.

When you forget a technical fix, go into your tips file and search for the title of the solution and you have the details in seconds— easy. I have about 30 pages of tech solutions.

> **Key takeaway: keep your own master recording system— a spreadsheet is okay for one to three VRs.**

CHAPTER 15

Risk Management

KEY POINTS

- Make a risk plan to mitigate all possible risks for your VR—and sleep well at night!
- Risk examples are shown.
- Be properly insured.
- Prepare appropriate terms and conditions for guests—some typical T&Cs are suggested.
- Security deposits are problematic.

Managing risk is a big topic, but in terms of basics, which this part of the book covers, there are some very simple things you can do to avoid major risks.

The simplest is to list all the things that can go wrong and have a solution to manage each of them. A few hours spent on this can forestall events that could put the entire business at risk. Here are a few examples so you get the idea. They are real examples from when I started operating Sea Zen. As we live in a remote town, lots of things can go wrong, but I am ready for anything.

Risk	Solution	Priority
Power failure	Information for guests, backup gas cooker, torches, how to get water when pump is off, etc.	High
Cleaner unavailable	Cleaner as a responsible partner. Encourage cleaner's own backup. Can owner do in emergency? Local backup cleaning service.	High
Treatment plant failure	Regular maintenance. Trained local person for emergency fix.	Medium
Owner incapacitated	Have a backup person trained to take over if owner is sick or on holiday.	High
Bushfire	Information. Emergency wi-fi. Bushfire app. Evacuation kit. Owner contact on high-risk days of year. Refund policy. (Real bushfire happened in 2015, guests safely evacuated.)	High
Damage by guest	Terms and conditions include responsibility for damage. Friendly personal greeting to subtly reinforce the unspoken message. "Friends of this small family look after the place."	High
Insect infestation	Information on insect screens.	Low
Only one mobile supplier network locally	Free backup mobile for guests with no network coverage.	Medium
Computer crash	Back up data onto the cloud—Dropbox.	High
Local rental restrictions	Ensure operating within local rules.	High
Guest can't operate rental facilities	Ensure simple "fix it" tips in information folder.	High

You can do a risk plan like this very quickly for the highest risks. You can also do a more in-depth plan later as your rental business develops.

As you can see, the example is for a remote town. If you operate an apartment in a city, there's an entirely different set of risks and solutions. You just design for your own risks.

Not only are you prepared, but also your guest will have a happier experience; you have pre-solved the problem and you will sleep soundly at night.

THE BUSHFIRE STORY

As our VRs were in a bushfire-prone area, I made a fire plan as part of our overall risk plan.

This involved insurance, an escape kit, guest awareness, a backup mobile phone, monitoring during high-risk days.

In December 2015, a devastating bushfire destroyed 118 houses in our village. I arranged for the guests in our two VRs to evacuate using our loan phones, just minutes after the fire warning. They made it to safety without harm.

One house was destroyed, another saved. The losses were well insured. I informed past loyal guests, and bookings were back to normal within months for the remaining property.

Owner incapacitation

As single owner-operators, what happens if you are sick or on holiday? You need a trained backup to keep the business running.

When a close friend and VR operator unexpectedly died, his untrained wife struggled badly for two years to keep the business afloat. A backup plan and training would have saved a lot of stress.

Insurance

You need to insure your structure and contents, public liability, and for guest damage.

What about cancellations from natural disasters? Some insurers have a travel insurance–like policy that guests can pay a little extra for to cover themselves against disasters and personal events. The policies seem to vary by country. My advice is to see a good local insurance broker to get the best advice on available insurance relevant to your country.

Terms and conditions

You need your own terms and conditions, particularly for your own bookings. These can be on your website, and at booking confirmation you can remind your guest that they apply. I like to put them at the back of the welcome pack I send to the new guest.

Typical conditions include:

- guest obligation to repay the cost of any damage, and for the owner to charge any such costs to the card on file
- guest to not have additional guests or overstay agreed dates
- no excessive noise, parties, or unauthorized visitors, no nuisance to neighbors, no illegal activities—guest to leave if they breach conditions
- cancellation policy, smoking policy
- fees for extra cleaning and excessive energy use
- pet request arrangements
- no guarantees of internet or other services beyond owner control, no helpdesk service
- owner welcomes any concerns as they arise, not after the event
- by payment of fee, guest has exclusive use but not possession
- any special local conditions.

What T&Cs should apply for online travel agency bookings?

There are standard OTA T&Cs that cover many of the above conditions. You can also add your own house rules. You should keep these simple, as you are in a comparative marketplace. If you have 20 lines of picky conditions and your competitors have just one or two phrases, prospective guests are unlikely to book with you.

What formalities for acceptance of T&Cs?

You should keep it simple. I've heard horror stories of owners sending long written contracts in the post to their guests and requesting they all be signed by all guests and mailed back. These days, you should simplify and state that proceeding with the booking will constitute acceptance of conditions.

If you are uncertain or if there are local laws that may require formal contracts, check with a lawyer familiar with local laws.

When you last stayed in a hotel, did they ask you to sign an elaborate contract, or any contract at all?

Security deposit

You have the option of asking for a security deposit. For some VRs exposed to risk, such as young groups, this may be wise. For routine stays, security deposits are problematic, as they require extra administrative steps at booking and in releasing the deposit afterwards. I don't bother, and I put more effort into forming a relationship with the new guest that makes them feel a welcome, responsible adult who has your interests at heart.

> Key takeaway: make a risk plan to mitigate all possible risks for your VR—and sleep well at night!

A Great Guest Experience

To get your guests wanting to come back and recommend you, they need to have a great experience. This starts the moment they inquire and ends the moment they leave. Every step should be effortless and enjoyable, like strolling down a gentle slope.

Here is a long list of examples. I use most of them, but you choose for your own business.

Before the guests arrive

- When inquiring, your images should be informative and enticing. If inquirers ask you questions, your answers are quick and informative.

- When they book, call them to answer any lingering questions and send them a valuable local **insider's guide** so they can plan their activities and anticipate the holiday in their imagination.
- Make it easy to find your property.
- If the property is ready early, they are offered a free early check-in.
- When they arrive, they can easily get the key to open the door.
- On some visits, they are met by the host personally, who makes them welcome.

When guests arrive

- As they open the door, they are greeted with welcome sensations. Soft music playing, a welcoming hamper or bottle of wine. A handwritten card of welcome. A pleasant scent. The view from the windows is even better than the images on the website.
- A welcome folder has an easy description of how everything works, from the wi-fi code to tips for the coffee machine. There is milk for coffee in the fridge.
- There are fluffy towels in the bathrooms, and soaps and shampoos. The house is spotless. The wood fire is set and lights at the first attempt. The reverse-cycle air conditioner is easy to use if the fire is not wanted.
- The beds are made up with fresh linen and attractive, with bright cushions. There are spare blankets in the wardrobes. The beds are very comfortable, and the guests have a good night's sleep.
- When it is time for a meal, the kitchen is well equipped, the knives are sharp. The appliances all work, and where helpful there are small labels making their use easy.
- There is information about the local shops and attractions in a folder, with road and transport maps.
- There are little extras to make the stay interesting. Books and images that complement the theme of the property. Games for the children.

- There is recreational equipment suited to the stay: fishing gear, bikes, etc.

Later in the stay

- For longer stays, leave a surprise like a bottle of bubbly or some local produce on around the third day.
- During the stay, the host sends a text checking if there is anything they need help with and reminding them of checkout time.
- There are small mementos of the visit to take home.
- When it's time to go, there is nothing to do except tidy up and close the door. An easy, memorable time away—expectations exceeded, lasting happy memories.
- The next day, the host asks the guest for a review (one click), reminds them they will get a special deal when they return and invites them to join the newsletter with local news and last-minute deals. See chapters 23 to 25 on newsletters for details.

Professional welcome folder

The key to an effortless stay is the simple set of information explaining how everything works. This may be an upmarket, simple, loose-leaf folder left in a prominent place that your guests can't miss. As well as helping your guests, it will reduce the number of times they need to contact you to solve simple problems.

A classic problem is guests switch the TV source from TV to DVD and can't understand how to get back to TV. A simple page with screenshots in your welcome folder will help them resolve the problem themselves in seconds—without having to contact you.

Less is more!

After your personalized welcome note in your welcome folder, add a simple index, in order of the things most likely to be needed, such as the wi-fi code. The instruction tips are in the same order as the index.

At the start, have the telephone number for the guests to call if they have any problems.

While you need to cover how most things work, for each item you need to be simple and brief in your folder. It's often possible to reduce four pages of an operating manual to just the four simple bullets in your folder that your guest needs.

The idea is to make everything easy. I often find that guests will pounce on the book as they arrive, skim it in a few minutes, and they are empowered to work everything easily for the rest of their vacation.

You can also leave "breadcrumbs" in the form of a tiny label at the appliance saying, "See info folder for instructions." If there is a key point for operating an appliance, use a Brother labeler to put just a few words at the appliance itself, and nothing in the welcome manual.

If you have a washing machine, look for the one-page instruction sheet in the manual, laminate it, and locate it next to the washing machine.

You might also have a separate folder listing local attractions and shops, which should be loose-leaf so you can add brochures and maps.

To app or not to app?

There are various excellent apps and iPad applications that provide the same function as the welcome folder; however, after many years of observing guests, it is clear that most guests do not want to learn a new technology while on holiday. The exception would be if your target audience is millennials, who prefer to get their information electronically. Like everything else, tune your offering to your target market.

> Keep it simple with a simple, well-curated folder.

The payoff—loyalty and reviews

You need to remember *why* you are giving your guest an exceptional experience. You want to earn their loyalty so they come back. You also need to earn 5-star reviews that you can use to boost your reputation and keep the online travel agency algorithms happy.

The reality is most inquirers will trust any kind of guest review far more than your claims.

A Nielsen study of 25,000 internet users from 50 countries (2009) found that 90% of consumers trusted recommendations from a friend, 70% trusted consumer opinions online, and only 33% trusted banner ads—i.e. you!

So it is a given that you should have a steady trickle of reviews to complement your description—at least one review a month—in your page on the listing sites. For an in-depth explanation of how to get the best from reviews, see Chapter 33: Guest Reviews in the Advanced part of this book.

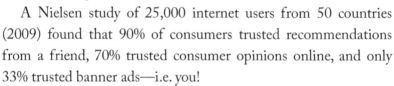

Key takeaway: systematically use standard processes to ensure a great guest experience.

CHAPTER 17

The Basics Quiz

How are you faring so far on your journey on the basics of VR rentals? Take the basics quiz here and check. I'd strongly recommend you do a reality check and get your basics right **before** you concentrate on the advanced parts.

Item	Implementation question	In place? Yes/Part/ No
Startup		
Regulations	Have you checked you meet local regulations for your rental?	
Servicing	Are there cleaners and tradespeople available in your area?	
Getting started		
Standard of finish	Does your VR at least meet the standards of internal finish for your local competitors?	
Beds	Are beds very comfortable?	
Kitchen	Is kitchen very well equipped?	
Neighbors	Do you have a close relationship with your neighbors in case of disturbances?	

Item	Implementation question	In place? Yes/Part/ No
Basic processes		
List on best websites	Have you identified the best websites to advertise for your local target market?	
	Are you advertising on the top three best websites?	
Photographs	Has your main hero shot been taken by a professional?	
	Do you have pics of every room, external, and a local attraction?	
Calendars and pricing	Are all your calendars 100% accurate?	
	Are your prices on par with your competition? (Okay to be lower first year getting started.)	
	Do you have a documented process to update each of your calendars, including bookmarks and passwords?	
Description	Does your VR have a simple, easily remembered name?	
	Is the name included in the headline description?	
	Is the description designed to appeal to your target customers?	

Item	Implementation question	In place? Yes/Part/ No
Cleaning	Have you created a close partnership with your cleaner, and do you pay them well?	
	Have you cleaned the property yourself?	
	Do you have a cleaning checklist that is used?	
	Do you have lockable cupboards for cleaning supplies to make your cleaner's job more efficient?	
	Do you have a way for the cleaner to view your forward cleans online, e.g. Google Docs?	
Back office	Do you have a system to record all bookings, all revenue, and all expenses?	
	Do you have a way of collecting card payments?	
	Have you identified your most serious business risks and a contingency plan for each of those risks?	
	Are you adequately insured?	
	Do you have securely filed lists of key information like appliances and manuals, your suppliers, documented processes, passwords, tech solutions?	

Item	Implementation question	In place? Yes/Part/ No
Guest experience	Do you have processes in place to ensure your guests have an enjoyable experience?	
	Are your guest processes at least as good as your competitors'?	
	Do you have a professional standard welcome book with basic information on how everything works, like wi-fi codes, etc.?	
	Do you have at least one good guest review per month of operation?	
Add up the number of yes answers (Only include Yes, not Part or No answers)		

HOW DID YOU SCORE?

Your score out of 30 questions	Where you stand on the basics
0–19	You have serious work to do to survive in the industry
20–24	A good start, but still a lot to do to get your basics right
25–30	Good work; time to start on the more advanced techniques

PART 3

ADVANCED TECHNIQUES FOR MASTERY

You need to get your basics right, as described in the previous part of the book, but in a competitive world, that will only get you so far. You will be just another commodity trying to compete.

Advanced techniques take you to the next level
The rest of this book describes a set of techniques that take you to the next level and high levels of occupancy.

They show you how you can stand out from your competition so more people find you and book your rental property. They also show you how you can use psychology to help persuade. Amaze them. Turn them into advocates. Encourage them to come back.

Focus on the important stuff
The key thing is to focus on the things that will be most effective on bringing you bookings.

The next chapter introduces, in a simple diagram, the trade-offs between impact of an activity in getting you bookings versus the effort involved. This **advanced techniques matrix** is used to set the scene for each chapter.

CHAPTER 18

The VRM Advanced Techniques Matrix

KEY POINTS

- Some techniques will give you high impact in getting bookings for small effort. Get to know which techniques to concentrate on first.
- As you read each chapter in this book, look to see the impact/effort trade-offs.
- Some techniques require considerable effort, but also will give you high-impact, lasting results. Choose the timing to suit your own improvement plan.

Focusing on the vital few

With all the tasks on offer, it can be overwhelming to improve your bookings. Owners can fast-track their journey to high occupancy if they focus on the vital few things that get the most impact. The dilemma is—what is important?

In this book I help a little by giving you an indicator of importance of each topic as you go. I do it by showing what the **impact** of each topic will be *and* how much **effort** will be involved. That way, you can do the easy ones that have the most impact early.

I use this diagram, which shows impact and effort for each topic:

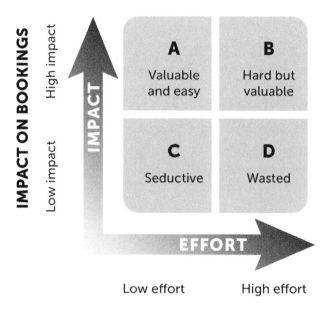

EFFORT REQUIRED TO IMPLEMENT

Zone A—valuable and easy

This is where the task is very effective at improving your bookings with little effort. The low-hanging fruit. These are the tasks you should do first. An example is getting a professional hero image to promote your listing that will result in many more bookings.

Zone B—hard but valuable

This is where the task has very high impact but requires considerable effort in terms of time, cost, or skills required. Intelligent forays into this zone can take you well ahead of your competitors.

An example is your newsletter to past guests, which will get you many more bookings but will take some learning to understand how to produce.

Zone C—seductive

This is where the task is easy and maybe even fun but does little to further your bookings. An example is a shopping spree to buy a colorful set of linens that you like but are impractical to launder and do little to grow bookings.

Zone D—wasted

This is where the task requires a lot of effort but does little to take your VR to the next level. An example might be spending two hours a day writing Facebook posts that result in few bookings.

The levels for each of the advanced steps are fairly subjective, being based on my 20 years of experience in the VR industry.

The **impact** is a combination of immediate bookings and long-term bookings.

The **effort** is a combination of time, cost, and degree of learning required.

Overall, it is a valuable guide to the differences in impact/effort for each task, to help you focus on the vital few. Here are the examples plotted on the chart:

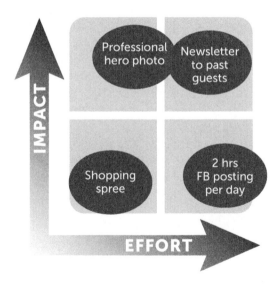

Where you see the impact effort matrix for an activity, you can use it to check how useful the activity is, so you can concentrate on implementing the vital few activities that will help you achieve mastery.

Plotting the advanced techniques

Unsurprisingly, most of the advanced techniques described in the next section are going to have high impact and a wide range of effort. Here are five examples plotted on the impact/effort matrix—my subjective assessment.

You can see that the mastermind activity is easily implemented and has high impact, whereas social media is seen as a high effort for not much impact. The idea is to give you a sense of which are easiest to implement and the degree of impact on getting bookings. Each chapter for each of the advanced techniques shows the impact matrix for that technique at the start.

Key takeaway: the VR impact matrix will help you identify high-impact techniques that get you bookings for small effort.

PART 3

**ADVANCED TECHNIQUES
FOR MASTERY**

SECTION 1

HUMAN MOTIVATION

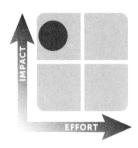

CHAPTER 19

Customer Feedback Obsession

> **KEY POINTS**
>
> - Systematically ask your guests about their experience at every step along their time with you to find ways of fine-tuning your offering. Nine touchpoint examples are given in the chapter.
> - Have a guestbook and a questionnaire in your VR to capture comments and suggestions.
> - If you offer more features than your competitors, make a list and tell inquiring guests.
> - Continuously improve your guests' experience.

A customer obsession can help you jump ahead of your competitors, and it can be fun! It is easy to do and it has a big payoff. You can know more about your guests' preferences as a group than they do themselves! Armed with this critical knowledge, you can design your VR experience to amaze and delight. You can turn guests into raving fans.

You can do it systematically. You can use the wisdom of crowdsourcing to sharpen your offering. This chapter shows you how, with lots of real-life examples.

Here are some guidelines for systematically uncovering your guests' needs:

- Use each guest touchpoint as an opportunity to listen to their deep needs.

- Ask high-value, open questions.
- Don't be intrusive in conversations; watch for warnings in body language and voice tone.
- A sample of a few questions for a few guests is all you need; don't overdo it.

> After a while you will develop deep knowledge of your guests' needs.

Let your guests design the experience

When I read some old reviews on my listing recently, there were two phrases that stood out repeatedly: Amazing attention to detail" and "You seem to have thought of everything!"

Oh, that's nice. I lucked out there. Or did I?

Actually, I didn't luck out. Nor did I have supernatural insights into future guest needs. Initially, there were few small details to delight my guests. I experimented. I listened, and **my guests told me** what they wanted. It didn't happen over weeks, it happened over years, and it's still happening.

The most valuable feedback was in the early months of operating, when I was too close to my own rental to see it fresh with the eyes of a guest. So I asked, in two ways, and still do.

- I had, and still have, a very simple paper questionnaire that asks for a rating on several attributes and an open question—how could we improve?
- As the guests were leaving, I "happened" to meet them[1], and I casually asked what they liked and didn't like.

> Ask your guests!

---

1   A movement sensor in the carport alerted us that they were leaving, and I took the dog for a walk!

The guests had lots of suggestions, and a few surprises, such as, "We loved the open-air hot tub." I explained I didn't have an open-air hot tub, just a spa inside. "Yes, you do. If you open the windows all around the spa and block off the inside with the screens, you have an outside hot tub watching the waves. Fabulous!" Of course! And that was how I promoted it on my website descriptions.

The guest suggestions tumbled out:

- a hook next to the shower
- some big fluffy towels and robes
- a shelf beside the vanity for make-up
- a light for the step at night
- a block-out blind for less light in the morning
- clearer instructions for connecting the DVD
- a list of walks
- a washing machine
- a bigger pantry
- a telescope
- and many more.

All were implemented. All were discovered by later guests who said we had thought of everything. This doesn't mean I implemented every suggestion. Sometimes I waited for a second suggestion, sometimes I checked with other guests. Some were just impractical or too hard. You, the owner, have to make the call.

There were many experimental improvements that the guests liked and some that they didn't like.

- "Loved the origami."
- "Loved the Japanese music CD."
- "Hubby went fishing with your rod."
- "Thanks for the maps."
- "Loved the food guide and the local tips."

I tried a range of local wines guests could buy, big effort by us to manage stocks. "No, we bring our own favorites." A romantic pamper package, big effort. "No, thanks."

I was nervous that my email newsletter might be too frequent for our return guests, so I asked. "Love it, can't wait to read it."

The competitive advantage—free extras

All my improvements added extra work for my cleaner, and one day she jolted me with an idea. *"You know that you do a whole lot more than my other cleans; it takes longer."* It was a light bulb moment.

I sat her down and checked what it was that we did extra. It was a lot. I started counting. There were over 35 extras that we provided for free that our competitors didn't, mainly because I was listening harder to our guests. I could use this in our marketing.

So I made a list that I could send to prospective guests who weren't sure if they would go ahead with the booking. I called it "The amazing 35 extras you get for free at Sea Zen." I put it on our Seazen.com.au website. You can download it yourself; it's still there.

I used the same approach on our earlier two VRs but refined our methods at Sea Zen. You can too.

Use guest touchpoints

Each guest touchpoint is a precious opportunity, partly a time for questions, partly a time to develop a relationship, as referred to in Chapter 22: Loyalty System.

Here are some ideas, but you can tune it to your own style for your guests.

Guest touchpoint	Typical questions/remarks (You should ask just one or two questions at a touchpoint; don't overdo it!)
Designing your VR before you start	Ask friends or guests at other VRs what they think of your concept/theme/name. Ask about alternative design concepts; which works best for them?
When the guest completes the booking by phone	How did you find us? Why did you choose us? What were you searching for? Can you remember the keywords you used? Is this for a special occasion? (If the booking was by email, you can make a "courtesy call" to see if they have any questions about the stay, and *then* ask them your questions!)
When the guest arrives	Can I tell you about the local area? Are you looking for anything specific? Let us know if we can help in any way.
The guest book	An opportunity for the guest to share their thoughts about their stay. Can be very emotionally evocative, can give insights into what other guests may subconsciously resonate with.
The brief questionnaire	A private way for the guest to tell the owner of any deficiencies or suggestions while still fresh.
During the stay	A check—usually by text—to see if there is anything the host can do. Will shake out any burning issues.
On departure	How did it go? How did you find [the latest experiment you are testing]? We're doing a random test—what was the best part of your stay? Just a favor—we're trying to get more reviews, is it okay for me to email you a link? Please tell your friends about your stay.

Guest touchpoint	Typical questions/remarks (You should ask just one or two questions at a touchpoint; don't overdo it!)
After they leave	(By email.) Thank you for your helpful suggestion about X; we have already planned to change X. I've just posted back your charger, etc. Thanks for telling us about the broken glasses ... etc.; no problem, we have lots of spares. You can leave a review here (link). You can also help our small business by telling your friends.
After they leave a review	Thank them.

Taking action

Little by little, you understand more and more about your guests' needs. Little by little, you modify your VR facilities and your VR experience to amaze and delight your guests so they become loyal return guests. They will say to you, "You have thought of everything!"

The really cool part about all this is it's fun and it's free!

> **Key takeaway: you can systematically improve your guests' experience via feedback.**

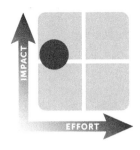

CHAPTER 20

The Psychology Of Influence

KEY POINTS

- There are six groups of psychological triggers to influence human behavior that can help get you more bookings: reciprocation, commitment, social proof, liking, authority, scarcity.
- Guests are happiest in the time before their holiday and during their most recent experience on their holiday. You can use this to help get reviews and repeat customers.
- There are ways to quickly establish rapport with guests and develop a better relationship.

We humans are strange people; we do the strangest things, and we are culturally programmed to do things that we don't want to! You can capitalize on humanity's psychological quirks to get more bookings for your vacation rental and have your guests love you for it. You are probably already exploiting some of these quirks unconsciously, but when I dig a little deeper in this section, you will uncover many tactics that you may not have heard of.

You can use the **psychology of influence** to help you to get happy guests, loyal guests, more bookings, higher rates, and ultimately a more rewarding business.

Bob Cialdini

The psychology of influence goes back a long way. In the 1980s a young psychology professor called Bob Cialdini in Arizona was intrigued by how salesmen often got him to buy something he didn't know he needed. Conventional psychology didn't explain why, so he went underground for three years, working for all kinds of salespeople, watching and learning. He found there was an underlying science of influence.

The result is a book he wrote in 1984 called *Influence: The Psychology of Persuasion*. It describes six principles that explain our unconscious programming and why we buy from one person and not from another. The book became an enduring success and sold over 3 million copies, topping best-seller lists with translation into 30 languages.

The principles are as true today as they were in 1984, and some you will recognize instantly, but they have subtlety.

THE SIX PRINCIPLES OF INFLUENCE:
- reciprocation
- commitment and consistency
- social proof
- liking
- authority
- scarcity

The challenge is knowing how to use each of these for your VR success, as shown below.

1. Reciprocation

As a young engineer working in Bangladesh in the 1970s, when visiting Calcutta I was given the bizarre task of buying 200 yards of the best calico cloth for our staff. Soon I was going from merchant to merchant looking at cloth. The cloth was all much the same, and I found it hard to decide on one. It was a very hot, steamy day, and despite me having had ample beverages, one skillful merchant persuaded me to accept a cold glass of Coca-Cola "to refresh Sir's thirst, no obligation, no obligation." I found myself accepting the drink, and I didn't buy his cloth, but I felt strangely uncomfortable leaving. I then went back and bought his cloth, which just happened to be about 10% over the market rate, but I felt happy. Afterwards I kicked myself for paying extra. What happened?

This illustrates the first principle of **reciprocation**. We are culturally programmed as a society to give to others and to return a gift with a gift. The size of the gift is not important; it will often elicit an obligation.

As another example, if a prospective guest calls asking about the local attractions near your rental at a time you are busy, you can brush them off or you can help them with a gift of your time.

It's a good tactic to help them. You may spend a few minutes on the phone. You may even have prepared a short guide to your area that you send them, a small gift. You don't make the hard sell; you just help. Let's say your caller has spoken to several other VR operators with similar prices, and you are the only one to help them; chances are they will feel a subconscious obligation. Chances are they will book with you.

As another example, you leave out a pot of local jam as your guests check in. You want nothing in return. Your guest is surprised and delighted. At the end of their stay, they think about the experience. The gift of jam is tiny, but strangely powerful. Chances are you will get a better review than without the pot of jam. Not always, but the odds are in your favor.

Later in the chapter there are several more tactics for each of the principles.

2. Commitment and consistency

In this principle, if a person makes a small effort in the direction of commitment, they are likely to make a consistent stronger move in the same direction.

> In a small town, the organizers of a fete asked some local shop owners to put up some large posters advertising the fete. Only a few owners agreed, most saying the signs were intrusive.
>
> The organizers approached a different strip of shops, and this time they asked if a small card could be put in the window advertising the fete. Most shop owners agreed. Closer to the date of the event, the organizers asked if a larger poster could go in the window, and this time most shop owners agreed. Having made a small step of commitment, the shop owners felt comfortable in continuing in the same direction with a bigger commitment.

Another example: a child sees a puppy in a pet store and says she wants it. Dad says we need to check at home with Mom, but the pet store owner says to just take the puppy and return it tomorrow if it doesn't work out. Of course, once the small commitment is made, a consistent commitment is made to keep the puppy.

As a VR example, a prospective guest says she would like to book but can't because she needs to check with her husband for his work availability. What I do in that situation is to say, "No problem.

I'll block out the calendar for you and you can tell me tomorrow if you would like to confirm." Most times they book the next day. A small commitment is made by the guest, followed by a consistent commitment the next day. Also, there is a small element of the reciprocation principle—the VR owner has made a small gift of blocking the calendar and the guest feels happy returning the favor with the booking.

Once a guest stays once at a VR, it's logical for consistency to keep returning—a return guest, year after year. We just help make it easy for them to enjoy that first and other experiences.

One of the reasons I like to have a guest book is that you often find guests writing that they enjoyed the experience, a small step of support. They are then more likely to recommend you to their friends—another step of consistency. They are also more likely to agree to write you a positive review.

A similar phenomenon is **confirmation bias**. Rather than people continuously testing their assumptions, it is more likely that they will form one viewpoint and assume it's true. That is good for you if they are a big fan of their experience staying with you and they tell others.

3. Social proof—the lead of the crowd

The term "social proof" has now entered everyday marketing, where people follow the lead of the crowd. Also, claims made by the crowd have higher credibility than claims made by the seller.

Have you noticed that at a public performance there is often someone in the audience who starts clapping when they appreciate a part of the performance, and sure enough *we* all follow suit and applaud. I suspect that may be a tactic by the organizers to garner more applause. Similarly, a sole person laughing will usually trigger wider laughter in the audience.

Paid applause became a business way back in 1820, when several opera fans offered applause during performances in return for payment. It worked and spawned a small industry of "claquing," where groups of people were paid for their appreciative response in the audience. There was a sliding payment scale starting from titters through to applause and even wild enthusiasm. Rent-a-crowd has been going for hundreds of years!

Cialdini points out that, faced with a new situation, folks will follow the lead of others in the crowd, and if everyone is waiting for everyone else to move, nothing happens.

After discovering this, Cialdini was later injured in a car accident, and folks stopped half-heartedly to see what was going on, then drove off. Severely injured, he found an onlooker at random and said, "You! Call the ambulance and divert the traffic." The startled onlooker did as asked, and other onlookers seeing the activity also stopped and helped. Cialdini had passed out by that time, and if he had not given a direct request, he may not have survived.

Again, folks needed another person to act for them to feel comfortable in acting.

> I was at the Airbnb Open in Paris in 2015 when terrorists shot scores of people in a suburb near my hotel, and much of Paris was locked down. Next morning at my hotel at 8 am, the streets were eerily empty. People were still stunned and had no signals as to what was okay. At 8.30 am, a few people ventured out in a trickle, then more. By 9 am the streets were bustling and back to normal. Once folks saw the signals that it was okay to go out, they followed each other. They followed the crowd.

As the most obvious VR example, a guest is far more likely to make a booking if there are already a lot of good reviews for the property. Guests often say, "We loved the picture and saw all the great reviews and decided to book."

> Reviews are our social proof—the VR currency of credentials

It always amazes me to see a long-running VR with just a handful of reviews. Without social proof, they will get far fewer bookings than their potential. Attracting steady reviews is one of the most important tasks for a VR owner, and it's free! In Chapter 33: Guest Reviews, I explain ways you can get steady reviews, and more of them.

> As another example, our guest book at Treetops attracted a new comment most weeks and soon became full, so I put out a new blank book. The new book stayed empty for a month, as no one wanted to be the first to comment. What to do? After personally asking several guests to help with a comment, there soon were three new entries, and the ball kept rolling with new comments every week from then on.

When renting a pet-friendly VR, there is a small risk that a dog may cause some damage. If I am welcoming a guest with a dog and I have an uncomfortable feeling about the guests, I use the power of the crowd to set expectations. "We are so lucky here; we find that guests who care enough about their dog to bring it along invariably look after our place." And it works. If the crowd is looking after the place, so usually will the new guests. It's all true; I just had to help the guest see what other people were doing.

Once you become very well booked, you can capitalize on that success as social proof. You can say in your description, "We are the most booked property in the area." The implied message is that the exceptional bookings are social proof that others are having an exceptional experience.

4. Liking

Liking is one of the basics of selling. Not in the sense of a superficial Facebook like, but in the sense of a human relationship.

People are more comfortable buying from people they like.

That is why Tupperware parties are so successful: guests are buying from friends. That is why companies have sales reps who visit their customers. It is why many folks buy a coffee from the same café where they are given a friendly welcome each day.

In operating a VR, we have lots of opportunities to develop a friendly relationship with our guests. Also, your guests will appreciate talking with someone they can relate to.

The inquiry stage is important. Sometimes an inquiring guest will ask about local places to eat. It's a natural opportunity for you to explain the features of the town, advice on where to shop and where not to shop, and so on. Soon you are a trusted friend, and more often than not the guest will go on to book.

We have lots of other opportunities to form a human relationship with our guests:

- If you are onsite, you can welcome and farewell.
- If not onsite, you can check mid-stay how they are going and if there is anything you can do.
- After they leave, you can call, thanking them for staying and, if appropriate, for leaving the place clean.
- If you have a newsletter, you can keep in touch with snippets of news in a friendly tone.

When deciding whether to review your VR, or whether to refer you to friends or whether to return to you, your guests will have more of an unconscious obligation if they feel a human relationship with you.

5. Authority

People are more likely to trust and follow someone with authority and do what they say.

If you have lived locally or even repeatedly visited for a long time, you have the authority of a local expert, so tell that to your guests on your profile page and your in-house information folder.

If you have an **insider's guide** to your area, it will be more highly regarded than something from Wikipedia, particularly if you have the authority of an insider. So you need to tell your guests in your guide about living locally. They are more likely to trust what you say, follow your recommendations, and be grateful for the experience. I've lost track of the number of times when departing guests have told me they've followed my recommendations and had a great time.

If you are active in supporting the local community, the tourism association or the local wildlife, your guests will respect you more. Again, tell them.

6. Scarcity

After countless studies, psychologists tell us that *we value something that we might lose more than something that we could obtain.* We have a fear of missing out. The result is that perceived scarcity generates demand.

You will have seen this used by salespeople in many situations:

- "Last one left."
- Bidders at an auction bid irrationally high because they don't want to miss out.
- "Last chance to buy today."

In the VR world, there are many ways you can use scarcity, but you should use it with integrity:

- A special offer to one person has a time limit—after which it is offered to someone else.
- A newsletter with a single special offered to many past guests creates competition.

- Calendar is filling fast—don't miss out.
- I've taken six bookings so far this week; bookings are very heavy, so don't miss out.
- This time of year, I get a lot of bookings and have to turn folks away—don't miss out.

Kahneman's observations on happiness

In addition to the influence principles from Bob Cialdini, there is another approach that you can use to enhance your guest experience, based on the work of Nobel laureate Daniel Kahneman. His work relating to the psychology of judgment is consistent with Bob Cialdini's view that we humans act irrationally. Here I discuss **happiness in vacation rentals** as described in an excellent TED talk by Kahneman (2010).

One of the periods of greatest happiness is the time leading up to the vacation, where the anticipation and dreaming give the guests a happy experience. My wife experiences just this for months when planning an overseas trip, though I leave this to her.

This is where your **insider's guide** can help with your guests' dreaming and planning. As this is just one person, maybe we should suggest our guest sends the insider's guide to the rest of the vacation party to maximize happiness?

Kahneman's studies also show that impressions of the vacation—and your rental—will fade within a few months of the stay, with just the peak memories lasting, which dominate the associated happiness for the vacation. Also, those memories are reinforced if guests tell others of their stay.

HOW VACATION HAPPINESS IS DECIDED

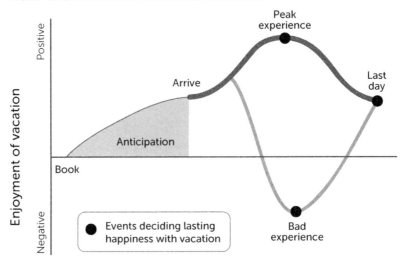

The most lasting impressions of the vacation are the most memorable event and the final day. If the most memorable event is a dispute or problem, that is what sticks. So resolving disputes happily will have a huge impact on the memory of the vacation and the association with your rental.

Asking a happy guest for a review will help your guest replay the memory of vacation and help reinforce their happiness.

Being onsite I often have a chance to see the guests toward the end of their vacation, often as they are leaving. It is quite common for the guests to be in a state of euphoria. "We've had just the most amazing time." They are almost floating! That's a perfect time to say you are glad and simply ask for that review, saying you'll send an email with a link.

The ecstatic guest is also likely to have left a joyous note in the guest book and the questionnaire, so if you are not onsite, your cleaner can text you a copy as she cleans, and you can send that email while the happy memories are fresh.

Expectations

Another principle (not from Cialdini) is that satisfaction is the difference between expectations and experience. That is why it's critical to accurately set expectations, so there is no disappointment with the reality. Better to under-promise and over-deliver.

A few little extras will also help exceed expectations and give you delighted guests and excellent reviews.

Another implication of expectations is that guests don't like negative surprises. Let's say that the coffee machine isn't working. If you leave it for your guest to discover the missing machine, they get a surprise, then go looking through your VR for all the other things that might go wrong. I have found from bitter experience that once on the hunt for problems, they will find more. On the other hand, if you set expectations by saying, "Sorry, the coffee machine will not be replaced until after your stay, but there is coffee plunger available," then the guest is happy. And the hunt for problems is avoided!

If your guest is after tranquility in their stay and there is noisy building work going on next door, you are better to set expectations and say there is some work going on. If they are aware and stay anyway, they know what to expect. On the other hand, if it's a concern, they are better off not staying this time. If you trick them into saying it is usually peaceful and they find the opposite, then you deserve a poor review and maybe a request for a refund. Clear expectations upfront will solve most problems!

Rapport through mirroring

Have you noticed sometimes that you are spellbound in a conversation with a stranger? I was first exposed to neurolinguistic programming way back in the 1980s, when I learned that people relate to others more positively if they use the same body language and word patterns.

How can you use this? If you are meeting a guest onsite, it helps them relax if you are using a similar stance to them; for example, if they are leaning to the left they will be more comfortable if you do too. They cross their legs, you do too. Somehow, they feel you are listening more intently and are more tuned in. These are small things, but they can be helpful in establishing rapport with your guests.

Also, people tend to use words relating to a pattern of sound, visuals, or touch, and if you use the same pattern, they will more closely relate to what you are saying.

If you are replying to a guest question where they use patterns of words involving visuals, then if you reply with the same pattern, you will make them feel more comfortable than if you use a different pattern. For example, if they ask, "I'm *looking* for a beautiful *view*, where I can *look* out to sea in the morning. I'd like to *see* if I can get a booking in March," they are using visual patterns, and your reply will resonate better if you use words around looking, seeing, etc. "Yes, you can *see* a great view. I'll *look* at my computer and *see* what dates we have free." Again, small things, but helpful with rapport, and they may just put you ahead of your competitors.

Matching emotional language in reviews and descriptions

As described in part 4 of Chapter 12, you can take the actual phrases used by happy guests and use the same words in your descriptions, where you can speak to potential guests who have the same hopes and wants.

For example, the review says, "The spa was sublime." Your description says, "You'll find the spa sublime." You tap into their deeper subconscious needs.

Using psychology

You are probably already using these various principles uncon-sciously to help get bookings, but now that you understand *why* these principles work, it can give you the extra confidence to use them more often—with integrity—to get bookings.

Like helping guests in the pre-booking stages (reciprocation), like forming a relationship with the guest (liking), like helping them have a great experience (reciprocation), like resolving issues quickly (reciprocation), like ensuring you get reviews (consistency and social proof). You get the idea.

> **Key takeaway: there are six groups of psychological triggers to influence human behavior that can help get you more bookings.**

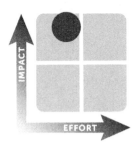

CHAPTER 21

Standing Out With A Theme

> **KEY POINTS**
>
> - Unless you find a point of difference to stand out from the competition, your VR will be forced into being a cut-price commodity.
>
> - A theme can help create a point of difference. Five examples are given of successful themes and a further 27 other theme ideas.
>
> - A distinctive name will help you stand out and be found on your own website for direct bookings.

Early in this book, I discussed how the online travel agencies have increased supply, thereby increasing competition. Most VRs have become commodities, pushing prices lower, and VRs are forced to compete on price. A decade ago you might have had 20 competitors. Now you might have a hundred or a thousand!

Renters are smart, well informed by the internet listings. If you are like your competitors, why should a renter choose you? If you're not careful you will be part of the commodity market, where logic says a smart renter will choose between equals based on price. As the simplicity of Airbnb continues to make it easy for anyone to list in your area, you will face more competitors, and soon it will be a race to the bottom based on price.

This section on standing out is really important. Things like conversion can be learned and systemized. Standing out is much more intuitive and much more important. It will jump you over the commodity trap. You can compete on experience rather than price.

Does your VR stand out?

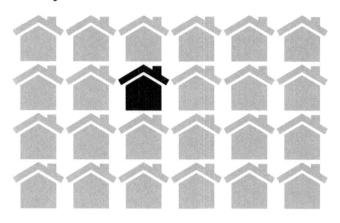

It takes risk, creativity, experiments, and persistence. Finding your difference is another small barrier. But, if you can break through the barrier, you will be far ahead of your competitors.

There are no easy answers, but this section has simple examples that can get the creative juices flowing.

Theme

It is worth spending a lot of creative thinking on how you can stand out. I like having a unique theme that will get your renters' attention. Once you have your theme, you can hang a lot of interesting experiences on it: the furniture, the decorations, the stories. If people come for the theme, price is less important in decision-making.

Sea Zen

When we made a sea change and built our new vacation rental, my wife and I agonized for weeks about what our theme would be. It could have been birds, fishing, shipwrecks, family pets, timber-cutting, native animals, and many more.

> We had been enthused for many years by Japanese culture and design, so it was easy for us to settle on a Japanese theme, focusing on the Zen of nature at the sea, and our "Sea Zen" theme was born. Once decided, everything fit with the theme, starting with the name. We designed huge Japanese shoji sliding doors. The furniture had a Japanese feel. The fabrics were Japanese. The prints on the wall were Japanese. Some Japanese crockery. Japanese books. CDs of traditional Japanese music. Books about Zen. A tiny book of Zen sayings.

Our hero shot features views of the sea, with the shoji screens to the side, over a view of the bed dressed with a fabulous red Japanese fabric. The photo stands out dramatically compared to the parade of competitor photos, which all look the same. People often say, "I love your photo."

It was an instant success, but did we luck into the only possible winning theme? Of course not, and any number of themes could work too.

Treetops

In the late 1990s, my wife bought a quirky three-level house in the rainforest, looking through large trees down to the sea, visited by rainforest birds.

"Treetops" aptly described this experience, and as we developed it for the market we played on the treetops theme. We moved the main bed so it looked out through branches and leaves to the sea.

You felt like you were in the treetops as you woke in the morning. We took photos of the rainforest birds and put them on the walls. We put bird books and binoculars in the bookcase.

We arranged a hero shot of the deck looking down to the sea through the tops of local trees, with local birds on the rail, gorgeous red flowers on the table, and the side of the house just in view. People said, "I loved your photo." They didn't know we took 19 of our own photos and three attempts by a professional before we chose one of our own. The name and the photo stood out from the competition. In time it became the most rented house in the area.

Steam

Our friends bought a property with a tired old railway carriage. They painted it in black and brass. They used a "steam punk" theme, with designs inspired by steam-powered machinery of yesteryear. Cheap, flashy brass fittings. Stainless steel sections. Wood panels. Crimson fabrics. Pictures of trains in their prime. You step into a new and fascinating world. Fun for kids and parents alike. Very easy to discuss with friends. The name "Steam" is simple and unforgettable.

It is one of the most rented properties in their town of Forrest.

Red graffiti wall

When looking for an apartment to stay in in New York, I found there were thousands to choose from, all similar. They were mostly small, with an image of a window looking out to other apartment blocks. Conservative images or no images on the walls. The one that stood out and is memorable years later had a full living room wall of bright red graffiti. Bold, over the top. Did we stay there? We wanted to, but it was already booked out!

Ipanema—retro shack

An enterprising young couple in our village bought an inexpensive old shack. Nothing much to look at but in a good location with a good view. It would be impractical to put in new windows or a fancy new kitchen and bathroom. Instead they decided to make the best of what they had. They decided on a general theme of '60s retro. They polished the floors. They fitted smart furnishings that stuck to the theme. Bookshelves filled with old books from the '60s. An old-style record turntable and lots of vinyl records. They gave it a retro name from the '60s—Ipanema. It has been very successful, and the aspect commented on with most affection is the old record player.

If you've got it, flaunt it!

Sometimes you already have a wonderful asset based on position. It may have a superb view. The ocean. The beach. The mountains. An idyllic stream. An adjacent vineyard. The city skyline. An iconic attraction. A historic building. A popular eating district. If you have one of these that stands out from competitors, use it for all it's worth and play on the asset as your theme.

Is it risky choosing an unusual theme? Sure is, but playing safe with everyone else is to be doomed to being a cut-price commodity, booked for the same fraction of the year as all plain rentals. If you pick a theme and it dies, no matter. You can easily choose another theme, new images, new story. You can update your website images and description in a few minutes. The internet is great for running experiments and finding a winner.

"Risky difference is a safer path to success than playing safe by being the same"

Choosing a theme

Preferably, it should be something that you are knowledgeable and passionate about. That way you will have the expertise, the energy, and the joy in developing your theme and sharing it with your guests. It will be something you love sharing rather than something you are bored with.

You should also consider your target market. What theme will get their attention?

Finding inspiration for a theme

So you have a good honest apartment with several bedrooms. It is bare and empty when you take possession. It is a blank canvas for your theme, but what to choose, where to go for ideas?

There is a rich source of ideas in the world of boutique hotels. These hotels had the same challenge as us in the VR industry—how to stand out in a crowded market? They have been using themes to stand out from their competition for the last few decades, and they have done it well. You can explore some and find styles and themes that you like. There are a lot in a wonderful collection on TripAdvisor called "London Themed Hotels." There are also a lot of pics of how professionals have styled the individual rooms. Dark colors, funky lights.

I trawled through various boutique hotels and found a treasure trove of themes.

Author, with pics, biography, and books	Musician, with lyrics printed on the walls	Local history, with pics and period furniture
Artist, with prints of their art	Pop art, with neon lights	Murals with paintings wrapping around the walls
Decade, with pics and music from an era—'30s, '60s, etc.	Movies, with huge posters from that movie in each room	Harry Potter
Willy Wonka	Autographs	Nautical, with models and images from an era
Alice in wonderland	Brewery	Sweatshop
Famous local identities	Minimalist	Olympics
Football	Toy collection	Red colors
Middle Eastern	Nature—plants	Nature—birds
Food—bread	Coffee	Icons—e.g. Eiffel Tower

So there are lots of ideas, but the most powerful theme is something you are really interested in so it's fun and not a burden, and new ideas come naturally.

You may have noticed that these themes have another nice outcome—a brand name. This is a nice handle for your loyalty system. It's also a nice handle to drive your own direct bookings on your own website. The name and its use are therefore extremely important.

As mentioned earlier, my wife and I spent a full day brainstorming hundreds of names before we settled on "Alto Richmond" for our inner-city VR.

Those local extras you offer

With a little creativity, you can offer local experiences that others don't. A local tour. A personal introduction to people and places that others won't find. Home-cooked pastry and jams. A special set of tips on the local fishing places. Tips on how to best play the local golf course. You can publicize these as a marketing attractor before guests stay, or you can provide them as a bonus that makes them raving fans.

This is most eloquently explained by Matt Landau in his "Limited Edition" series, examples of what creative owners from around the world have achieved by finding and flaunting a distinctive difference. You can see the series if you are in Matt's "Inner Circle."

> **Key takeaway: unless you find a point of difference to stand out from the competition, such as a distinctive theme, your VR will be forced into being a cut-price commodity.**

PART 3

ADVANCED TECHNIQUES FOR MASTERY

SECTION 2

CORE PROCESSES FOR MASTERY

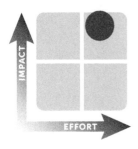

CHAPTER 22

Loyalty System

> **KEY POINTS**
> - Small VR owners have a big advantage over online travel agencies—their personal relationship with their guests, the basis of a loyalty scheme.
> - Past guests need to be able to find you—use a memorable VR name.
> - A newsletter will help you stay in touch with past guests.

The reality is VRs are dominated by large online travel agency platforms like Airbnb, Booking.com and Expedia. Many vacation rental owners despair about this domination. "How can a small person compete?" We all need to remember that we small vacation rentals actually have a huge advantage over the OTAs. *We have a personal relationship with our rental guests that no OTA can ever match.*

> VR owners have a personal relationship with guests that no OTA can match

This is particularly true when your guests keep coming back to your area. Same summer holiday. Same anniversary celebration. Same local family to visit. Same sporting events to attend. Same deep inner need to get away from the city to a favorite refuge to recharge the batteries.

If you are part of a repeat market, a loyalty system is the most effective way you can bring guests back to *your* rental, and they book direct. A loyalty system can also save you huge marketing commissions paid to the big online travel agencies. You are in control.

A loyalty system is one of the most important things you can implement if you want high occupancy and vacation rental mastery.

"THEY NEVER MADE CONTACT"

A friend, Michelle, said to me that she once had a fabulous holiday at Lorne near our rental, but she never went back, choosing instead to go to a closer place for holidays.

I asked why.

"We had a fabulous holiday at this nice place, but *they never made contact*, and I simply forgot about them!"

How many of your past guests loved their stay and simply forgot about you?

A loyalty scheme keeps guests in touch and keeps you on their radar, keeps them from forgetting about you. Yours is the first name they think of for their holiday. An easy solution for your guests.

What is involved in a loyalty system?

- a great initial experience worth repeating
- a relationship
- raving fans—we hope!
- an email address
- value
- a brand name
- takeaway reminders
- easy to book—on your website
- reminders via a newsletter—this is the clincher!

Loyalty—a great initial experience worth repeating

When your guests stay at your property, you should be aiming to make it a fabulous experience. One that messes with their heads (nicely) enough to remember you.

There are whole books written on how to do this. You make a lovely place to stay. All the basic facilities they want. Special extras to surprise and delight and to tell their friends about. Everything easy to use. If something goes wrong, a quick response that makes them feel special. I described how to do just that in Chapter 16: A Great Guest Experience, way back in Basics.

Loyalty—a relationship

> "A relationship sells"

This is where you shine. Sooner or later in the booking process you have a chance to say hello and inject your personality. While booking you can speak with them. (Yes, actually speak with them!) You may be able to greet them as they arrive. During the stay you can check if everything is okay. At the end of the stay you can (should) ask how they found the experience. They know from their experience that you are a nice person. Someone worth remembering. Someone they can tell their friends about. This resonates exactly with the "liking" principle explained earlier in the Psychology section.

At the end of the experience, they know you and you know them. Often face to face. Mostly by telephone. Always by email. Can the online travel agencies have this relationship? Never. This is where you excel. *This is your unfair advantage over the OTAs.* Use it.

Loyalty—one hundred raving fans are a business!

So you have given your guests a fabulous experience, and you have a warm relationship. Not all, but *some* of these guests will become raving fans and tell all their friends about your rental. They love the experience and will come back every year or two. They will get a friend to come every year or two. Each of these fans will give you about one booking per year ongoing. You need to build up your raving fans year after year.

In an early chapter I showed that for an average three-night stay, and 90% occupancy, you will get about 110 stays per year. If you can get 100 raving fans, they will give you 100 stays per year, close to the 110 maximum possible. This loyalty stuff works!

> Six years ago, I met a couple who ran three pet-friendly stone cottages on a rugged farm overlooking the wild ocean just meters below. We agreed to compare our VR rentals. I asked them about their operation, which online travel agencies they were using, their advertising offline, and so on. I was surprised when they were vague in all their answers. Finally, I asked about their occupancy, and they said around 90% and the calendars were full, as usual. It suddenly became clear they had a huge following of raving fans who kept coming back. The owners didn't advertise; their fans just called them and booked in. I recently checked their calendars, and it still has the same high bookings. These businesses do exist!

How do you build raving fans? One at a time. Rather than seeing how quickly you can complete the booking transaction, take your time with your guests and get to know them and what they are looking for in their holiday and how you can help them.

If you are listening to your guests, you will have refined your VR property so they have a truly exceptional experience. Some of them will become raving fans.

Getting your guests' email addresses

I'm often asked, "How can I get their email address? All their details are hidden behind the online travel agency curtain!"

Simple. I have 100% success in getting all my guests' personal emails and telephone numbers. You can too. You exchange entry and local guides for their email.

After booking, your guests need to be able to get into your vacation rental. You control this. They need the map, the key, the address, the combination to the keylock, the special instructions to get in, sometimes a meeting place and time to be let in. In almost all cases, the online travel agencies need to give you the guest's telephone number so you can let them in.

You text them asking for their personal email so you can send them your map and welcome pack and—this is important—your unique local information and tips. You tell them you can't send it through the online travel agency mail system because that often strips out attachments, so you prefer to send it to their direct email address.

Remember, it is *your* vacation rental. The OTAs are being paid for the introduction to your guest. You are not some monkey turning somersaults for the OTAs to provide unknown guests who may damage your property. You are in charge; remember it.

Loyalty—value to both parties

A loyalty system is a value exchange. You have guests coming back, booking direct and saving you an online travel agency commission. They will probably tell their friends if you play your cards right, and they will also book direct. Your occupancy increases. These are three different sources of **value to you.**

You also have a responsibility to provide extra **value to them.**

You can give them special discount for booking direct. This can also apply to their friends booking direct with you. It may be a 5%–10% discount or $50 off, whatever feels right for them and you.

I have a small card that guests can take away and give to their friends, telling them about the discount. You can make them *feel* special and valued. You should be genuinely excited to have them re-book with you. You should be warm in your contact and thank them for coming back. If you have a greeting card when guests arrive back at your rental, it should also thank them for returning. You can give them little extras for returning. In our case, I provide returning guests with Japanese robes or a bottle of sparkling wine. You can figure out what small extra gift you can give them that is appropriate to your rental and your area. Maybe you make home-made jam, or you can give them some local produce.

In the paragraph above you can see three examples of value to you and three examples of value to them. You can have some fun in finding what works for your guests.

Loyalty—a memorable brand name

I'd like to reinforce the importance of a strong brand name for your VR. Given its importance, it is worth considering again in the context of loyalty.

You want your past guests to come back. You want their friends to be able to find you. It should be easy to find your website if you have one. *You are in a battle for people's memories.* Therefore, you should have a short, locally unique name that is easy to remember. Ideally, it may say something about your unique offering, but that is far less important than having something memorable. Chapter 11 goes into how to choose a good name. If you haven't yet got a name for your VR, go back to that chapter.

A logo

Don't fall into the trap of investing extensively in logos and corporate designs associated with your brand name. A logo is a nice thing to have, but way down there in the importance stakes. If you want an image, you can use your hero shot repeatedly. If a logo is associated with your name and theme, that's nice, but not worth tying yourself in knots over.

I always leave a hero shot at the footer of my booking confirmation email—time taken: five seconds; cost: nil; recognition: high.

It would be 10 times more important to spend a day setting up a simple email newsletter than spending a few days and $1,000 getting a graphic designer to give you a logo.

Once you have your brand name clear, you can use a logo to look more professional and help past guests find you through your website. There are some tips on easily getting a logo in Chapter 51: Tips and Hacks.

Reminders

You can help guests depart with handy reminders. I have a business card–size loyalty card and a branded pen. Other enterprising owners give them branded souvenirs. A branded cap, branded pen, branded fridge magnet. There is a lot to choose from, and inexpensive if they save you an expensive online travel agency commission. Just don't do cheap and tacky.

Loyalty—easy to book on your website

So, let's say your guests love your rental and tell their friends, who want to book. They can find you on the web.

If you have your own website, they can book direct with you there. When they do, it should be easy—via a booking calendar or an invitation to call you direct. It should be as easy as walking down a gentle slope to a welcoming café. Better that it's your own website rather than your listing on an online travel agency site, where you pay those high commissions. For example, if you have a rental called Red Door and it is located at Lorne, your website might be called www.reddoorlorne.com, for example. Just keep it simple.

Some vacation rental owners are intimidated at the prospect of getting their own website. The effort and the cost can be considerable, but if you are well informed it can be simple, inexpensive, and safe. It is also getting easier. I'll have more to say on that later.

Loyalty—reminders via your newsletter

So now your guests have had a great experience, they know you and they like you—and you have their email address. Chances are they will come back for a holiday in your area. What you need to do next is simple—stay in touch.

The best method is to send them an email. This is by far the most effective way of helping your guest return to you. This in turn increases occupancy, reduces external commissions, and increases your margin. Many owners who are well on the path to vacation rental mastery have an effective email marketing system.

If you are in a transient market where visitors are unlikely to return, an email marketing system has lower effectiveness. But don't give up; chances are they enjoyed their holiday enough to tell their friends, and your email marketing system will help reach those too.

Email marketing via a newsletter is such an important topic it deserves its own section in this book. You might even want to get a separate book or training course, but the basics are simple.

> Key takeaway: small VR owners have a big advantage over online travel agencies—their personal relationship with their guests.

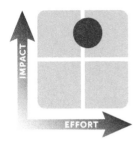

CHAPTER 23

Guest Newsletter —Examples

> **KEY POINTS**
> - Getting started is the hardest part.
> - Guests will love your newsletter if you make it informative and entertaining.
> - Keep all guest email addresses, even if you aren't ready to send the newsletter just yet.
> - Get guests' permission to email them.
> - A simple and a longer newsletter example are shown.

The most valuable part of my VR business —the newsletter

After more than 20 years in the holiday rental business, when I think back to all the marketing experiments and failures I have tried, **the newsletter is by far the most effective at getting bookings,** and with zero cost other than time. My only regret is that I didn't do it earlier.

As part of your loyalty program, you need to **keep in touch** efficiently in a way that your guests enjoy, and make it easy to for them to book. Sounds easy.

Your biggest challenge for newsletters—starting!

For most owners, the biggest challenge is getting started. For many the obstacle is fear, whether it's the fear of failure, fear it will be too complicated, or fear of alienating your guests. Everyone feels it.

This is actually good news; it is a barrier of entry that your competitors will also feel. Once you're through it and have mastered email newsletters, you will be well ahead of your competition.

One of the biggest votes of reassurance came to me when I spoke with a past guest who booked after a newsletter. I asked her what she thought of our newsletter emails. She told me how much she looked forward to getting them and staying in touch with what was happening down in Wye River. That has been repeated every time I have asked a past guest for their opinion about our newsletter.

So, feel the fear, take a deep breath and do it anyway; it isn't very hard!

Length warning!

As this part is particularly valuable for those who wish to start their own guest newsletter, I've included practical information on how you can get started and divided it into three chapters—Examples, Choosing a System, and Maximizing Readership.

> Examples → Choosing a system → Maximizing Readership

If it's not for you, skip to the chapters on websites, beginning at Chapter 26.

Will past guests like your newsletters?

The key to starting to email past guests is understanding that they *will* appreciate your newsletters, provided you keep them informative and entertaining. After many checks over the years, I've been astounded at the number of past guests who not only like my newsletters, they tell me they actually look forward to getting them.

Overview of newsletter system

THE STEPS INVOLVED IN NEWSLETTER SYSTEM
- Capture the email address.
- Write the newsletter so it gives value to your past guests (examples below).
- Use technology for an efficient email delivery process.
- Refine for effectiveness.

Capture the email address

The prior section of this book has tips for capturing email addresses when the big online travel agencies try to block that address. In a nutshell, you don't give them access to stay until you have their personal email address.

Permission

Due to spam regulations, you should also get the guest's permission to put them on an email list. I like to call the guest after they stay, thank them for staying and ask if they would like our newsletter, which other guests overwhelmingly enjoy, and you can unsubscribe any time. Everyone says yes.

A recurring problem is owners aren't sure if they will have a newsletter, so many don't bother keeping guest details in an orderly list, thinking they can go back and collect emails later. It is best to collect details upfront, when it's easy. Airbnb and Booking.com remove old email addresses and telephone numbers, so you may have big gaps in your data. It is also good to get opt-ins when everything is fresh.

Getting opt-ins from past guests

What if you have a list of 300 past guests but you haven't got their permission to send them a newsletter?

Just ask them as a follow-up from the time they stayed with you whether they would like to get the newsletter, and most will say yes.

A recent experiment by another owner, Zoe, found 90% of recent guests were happy to opt in and several were even interested in booking again. Guests of several years ago are less likely to opt in.

Master list of information

Next you need a master list of past guest information. A simple spreadsheet will do, and often your own booking records will suffice. If you use email software, then periodically, typically once a month, you transfer the key information into your emailing system.

What to store?

You need to include key information that you can use for the newsletter. This typically includes:

* email address—crucial
* first name—desirable so you can personalize your message.

You should also consider keeping other important information that you can use to segment out different groupings with different messages in the future. More on that later.

Write the newsletter—so it gives value to your past guests

You want your guests to read your email and to keep reading future emails.

Here's my formula to give your guests value:

* some local news
* some interesting pics relating to your news
* a special offer that would be valuable to them
* a reminder that past guests get a discount or benefit
* a link to the booking calendar

- how to unsubscribe
- keep the whole thing brief
- make your subject line interesting.

You don't want it to be "salesy." It should be interesting or entertaining or informative, so they read it and your VR gets back in their mind.

> The acid test is this: would you find that newsletter interesting if you were a guest?

Everyone loves a story, and true local stories are always a good read. A good topic is local news. Let's face it: your guest liked your area enough to stay there with you, so they are probably interested in what's happening down there when they are back home dealing with life.

Most people like a bargain, and most of your guests will too. You might offer a special deal on particular dates. The dates may not suit your readers this time, but they are more likely to open the email next time if they have the chance of a bargain deal to suit their plans.

You should give them a link to your calendar to make it easy to see the dates they can book. Some email systems can even tell you who has clicked on that calendar link, and you can send a follow-up email if you like.

You should remind readers of any special benefits that past guests will receive when they return. I give them a small discount and an extra, like loan Japanese robes that other guests do not get, so past guests really do get a unique deal.

You may even choose to invite them to a further value-add—to be added to a special "last-minute" list, for the few who like to chase a bargain on a last-minute vacancy. This is another opportunity for you to fill a few days in your calendar that would otherwise be vacant.

An "unsubscribe" link is essential. Most countries have laws that require you to allow your recipients to unsubscribe from your emails. It's just courtesy anyway. Paradoxically, if your guests know they can unsubscribe easily anytime, they are more likely to stay subscribed, as they know they are in control.

Brevity is important so your recipients can scan the newsletter in seconds and read deeper if they want. If you ramble so it takes a while for your readers to understand the gist of your email, they are far more likely to unsubscribe. A way to keep it brief and allow those interested to read a lot more is to have a "read more" link to a more extensive article on your website. (That article can also help make your website more attractive to Google for long-tail search terms and SEO, but that is a whole separate topic.)

Your subject line is as important as the body of your newsletter, in terms of getting your email opened. It should be interesting, but it should not use terms that get it trapped in your past guests' spam filters.

Learning by example

You can see from real examples how it all works. You can see the simple and the mature versions of a real email. Both work. You can start simple and grow.

The simple email newsletter

Just have one story, a special deal, a link to a calendar, and a way to unsubscribe manually. It will be almost as effective as the more extended mature version and is a great way to start out. You can send via BCC using your normal email software like Gmail or Outlook. You can manage the distribution list manually and remove the unsubscribes manually.

Example of a simple newsletter sent manually to an email list using your normal email software

---

Subject: "Sea Zen—introducing gannets, ballerinas and killers."

The aerial ballet

Many days at Wye River we are treated to an aerial ballet of the gannets. They circle out to sea like graceful ballerinas, until they spot a fish below. Then they turn into deadly killing machines, plunging into the water at over 100 km/h!

Here is the transformation from glider to killing machine.

When they are around, we can watch them for hours through the binoculars!

These are one of the most fascinating birds ever. You never know what birds you will see at Sea Zen!

August Crazy Special—half price

Stay 2 days half price—Thurs 17 Aug and Fri 18 Aug.
Normally $686, now $343 just for our past guests. First to book.
Call me on 0412 345 678 or email rex@seazen.com.au

Bookings

For bookings, you can call me or book online here. [link to online calendar]

Don't forget that return guests booking direct with me enjoy a $50 discount. We also add little extras for return guests, extras like a bottle of Gluhwein in August.

In Zen

Rex and Sibylle

To unsubscribe, just reply saying you would like to unsubscribe.

Anyone can write this simple email above and send it out manually, with no software.

The mature newsletter version

An extra local news story is added along with about three small images overall. There is a link to a richer story on the website for SEO. There is an invitation to join an exclusive last-minute list. There are links to past stories. There is a footer added by the email software to automate unsubscribes.

Example of an actual newsletter I sent to my past guests. It has two brief news stories and one special offer

---

Subject: "Sea Zen—introducing gannets, ballerinas and killers."

Hi Leanne [personalized to each past guest]

The aerial ballet

Many days at Wye River we are treated to an aerial ballet of the gannets. They circle out to sea like graceful ballerinas, until they spot a fish below. Then they turn into deadly killing machines, plunging into the water at over 100km/h !

Here is the transformation from glider to killing machine.

When they are around, we can watch them for hours through the binoculars!

These are one of the most fascinating birds ever. Read the full story here [link to longer story on my website for SEO].

George is back!

Our random visiting koala, George, wandered back last week. Here is a pic of him nearly invisible in the tree, just five meters from the Sea Zen balcony

August Crazy Special—half price

Stay 2 days half price—Thurs 17 Aug and Fri 18 Aug.
Normally $686, now $343 just for our past guests. First to book.
Call me on 0412 345 678 or email rex@seazen.com.au

Bookings

For bookings, you can book online here. [link to calendar]

Don't forget that return guests booking direct with me enjoy a $50 discount. We also add little extras for return guests, extras like a bottle of Gluhwein in August.

Exclusive last-minute list

We have an exclusive email list of 32 past guests for last-minute discount offers—let me know if you'd like to be added to the list.

In Zen

Rex and Sibylle

Some popular past stories you might like:

[links to nine prior stories on Sea Zen website]

After the email—just take the bookings?

You may get bookings immediately after the email, but you may not. The special offer is often booked within hours of the email, with several past guests missing out.

You should not be discouraged when there are no bookings in the days after a newsletter is sent. I learned over the years that I do get the bookings, but they come in dribs and drabs in weeks and months after the newsletter. Emails would come in as direct replies to the newsletter email, sometimes months later: "I've been thinking about coming back for a while, can I book for these dates?" The newsletter achieves the primary aim—**keeping in touch; keeping in top of mind**.

> Key takeaway: guests will love your newsletter if you make it informative and entertaining.

CHAPTER 24

Guest Newsletter— Choosing A System

> **KEY POINTS**
> - Three alternative approaches to sending newsletters are compared—manual, outsourced, automated.
> - Four automated system vendors are compared.

Technology for an efficient email delivery process

You will notice that in the prior chapter I talked about how I provide value for our past guests in our newsletter *before* I even think about the technology tools.

Some vacation rental owners start with the delivery technology and get overwhelmed and lose sight of the value-add. You can start simple and add the technology later.

Broadly speaking, there are three alternative email delivery technologies:
- a simple manual email
- an outsourced service to someone who handles it all for you
- automated software like Mailchimp.

In each case, *you* write the email. The difference is just how emails get to your readers.

COMPARISON OF DELIVERY APPROACHES

Manual email	Outsourced	Automated email software
Emails are sent to your list from your email system.	A commercial service takes your email, manages your list, and sends the emails.	Automated software to compose, send, and manage responses. Mailchimp is the example used in this table.
Price Free	**Price** Price—typically $30/mo. for 2,000 subscribers	**Price** Free for list of under 2,000 subscribers
Pros • simple, uses existing technology • easy to get started, no special learning needed **Cons** • can't personalize the email • formatting is clunky, e.g. pics can be tricky to add • can look amateurish on mobiles • manual unsubscribes can be tedious • hard to send to segments • lower response rates	**Pros** • someone else handles all the technology • no learning curve **Cons** • price • can be hard to find the right supplier • you still need to write the story and provide the list of guest emails. • loss of control • delay from story to emails sent	**Pros** • sending and unsubscribes are automated for you • newsletters look professional • photos easy to include • easy to add subscribers from a spreadsheet • handy reports track opens and clicks to measure effectiveness • can send to segments • your newsletter can look good on both mobile device and desktop **Cons** • can be confusing to choose a suitable software supplier • free version usually has logo of provider in footer

Manual email	Outsourced	Automated email software
Suited for • starting out, with a list of 20–50 past guests • owners with just one rental	**Suited for** • owners who hate learning new technology and are happy to pay someone else to do it for them	**Suited for** • volumes over 50 subscribers • owners who like to DIY • owners who like control

Simple technology—manual emails

You can use the simplest of technology when you are starting out. You write your email and just send it out from your normal email program to your list of email addresses. It works well when you have a relatively small list of, say, 20–50 past guests.

It must be sent BCC, so no one sees all the other email addresses. You just compose the email, put all the email addresses into the BCC box and press send.

You must also include a way to unsubscribe. "To unsubscribe, just reply saying you would like to unsubscribe." You then need to reply, confirming you have taken them from your list. Easy for a small list.

The big advantage is if you are action-oriented, you can get started with manual emails immediately. You can "just do it"! And it's free.

The limitations of a manual system are:
- You need to manually manage the unsubscribes and closed email addresses.
- You can't personalize to each recipient, e.g. "Hi Leanne, …"
- Formatting, e.g. images within the email, is fiddly.
- It can look poor on mobiles.
- It is harder to send an email to specific segments, e.g. families.
- You get lower response rates than other methods.

As your list expands, you will need to use a system that can cope with the higher volumes.

Outsourcing of newsletters

It might sound strange to outsource emails; after all, we all send emails every day. But we need to acknowledge that sending email campaigns to past guests comes with some challenges.

If someone can get the technical stuff right, your newsletters will look good and you will get a higher response rate. That is what you want from a loyalty system. You can spend your time thinking of emails that add value for your guests. Someone else does the technical stuff.

There are good services out there that do all the technical stuff. You send them your email text and the email addresses, and they do the rest. Typical costs are $30–$50 per month. One such service is www.market2all.com, and there are many more.

Is this right for you? It depends on whether you like to avoid new tools and have others do the technology thing or whether you like to embrace new tools and experiment yourself. It is a personal style thing.

My wife—who can write fabulous emails—prefers others to do the technology thing. On the other hand, I like to try out new tools and run lots of experiments.

There is no right or wrong here. The great thing is that you have a choice. You decide.

Automated email software

Let's say that you choose (like me) to use automated software to send your emails. Some years ago, I chose Mailchimp, and it is free and well known in the industry. It has pros and cons compared to competitors, but it works for me. Most software will do similar functions.

I have used **Mailchimp** as the example here, and the kinds of functions that it automates.

What can email software do for you?

- Manage your list of past guests.
- Organize a "campaign" and format your email.
- Send the email to your target audience.
- Report on outcomes.
- Automatically manage unsubscribes and dead emails.

Managing your list

You tell the software the attributes that you will store for each past guest. It can be as simple as just the email address. The guests' first names are helpful to include so your emails are more personal.

As an example, after many years of customizing to my VR operation, I like to keep seven fields: email address, first name, date of first stay, pet ownership, repeat guest status, last-minute list, property stayed at. I have the base data stored in my own spreadsheet, uploaded to the email software. You may want to keep the bare essentials like email address; you decide.

Then you upload your spreadsheet into the system. It makes it easy for you. For example, you can upload your spreadsheet of guest details in a few seconds, no copy and pasting of individual fields.

At the end of the month you can add the extra 10 or so new guest details in the same way.

If someone unsubscribes or their email stops working, the system handles it all; you don't need to do anything.

If you want to, you can create a target segment. I have one called "Last-minute" for those who asked to see my last-minute specials.

Initially, you should keep it simple and just send to your entire list.

Organizing your email or campaign

You name your "campaign"—for example, "August newsletter"—and create a subject line.

You choose an existing template or make a new one, and type in your newsletter wording. You can add photos, headings and links and even different fonts, but my suggestion is **you keep it as simple as possible**.

Mobile considerations

Most of your audience will read your email on their mobile. There is nothing worse than a tiny font your guests can't see on their mobile, or a huge font that's clunky and unreadable. Guests will delete the email after about a second if it's hard to read. A very helpful feature of the email software is the ability to make your email size different for desktops and mobiles, so your audience sees it at a nice size no matter what device they choose. More readership = more bookings.

Sending your newsletter

You should always, always, always send yourself a final test email to see how it looks on desktop and mobile. A good email will enhance your brand, and a bad email will degrade your brand and undo all your hard work. Once you are happy, you can send then or schedule it to be sent another time.

Reporting on outcomes

The software will tell you in real time how many recipients have opened your precious email and—horrors—the small number who have unsubscribed!

You may find, like I do, that it's exciting to see the campaign unfold in the minutes and hours after the email is sent.

You can track how your latest newsletter compares to previous newsletters. The trend in proportion of emails that are opened. The trend in the number of clicks. You can see which links have been clicked and even by whom. Are they clicking to check your calendar for a possible booking? You can even see which stories are most popular.

You can also see trends in the opening of emails. A decline may mean you are emailing too frequently. If so, time to back off a bit. I discuss frequency in the next chapter.

Reporting is one of the real strengths of email software. That alone may be a good reason to invest the time and effort in automated email software.

Choosing automated email software

There are scores of automated email systems out there, each with their own strengths, each fiercely looking to establish their own territory. The more powerful they are, the more complex to understand and use. There is some value in keeping it simple.

They are in two broad groups:

- **basic emailers** with a good range of options for sending and reporting
- **sophisticated marketing systems** that can send emails depending on various conditions, typically designed for marketing funnels. They combine sales, marketing and customer contact

For the target readership of this guide, i.e. vacation rental owners with one or a few vacation rental properties, basic email systems will be the most appropriate.

The table below summarizes the various options for email software.

System type	Examples and pricing	Selection comment
Basic emailers	Mailchimp • versatile software, simple, searchable help • well-established, with free entry option, compatible with Wordpress.com • 0–2,000 subscribers free* • 2,000–2,500 subscribers $360 p.a.*	• a good option for small VR operators • used by author of this book
	AWeber • versatile software, simple, access to rep. • 0–500 subscribers $200 p.a.* • 500–2,500 subscribers $300 p.a.*	Similar to Mailchimp
	Constant Contact • versatile software, simple, access to rep. • 0–500 subscribers $200 p.a.* • 500–2,500 subscribers $450 p.a.*	Similar to Mailchimp
Marketing systems	Infusionsoft • integrated marketing system including email • essentials plan $2,400 p.a.*	More features than needed by most VR owners
*USD, 2017 pricing with annual discount; all have free trial period.		

There are useful articles comparing the popular systems. Google "compare mailchimp aweber constant contact" for the latest comparisons.

Key takeaway: you have several viable platforms for sending newsletters.

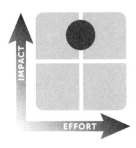

CHAPTER 25

Guest Newsletter— Maximizing Readership

> **KEY POINTS**
> - Five ways are given to maximize readership.
> - Over 20 example topics are given to show there is a huge number of topics suitable for your newsletter.
> - A newsletter can be the most powerful source of repeat guests.

This chapter has tips and advice on going to the next level with email marketing to get read—and the best results.

Maximizing readership

Subject line

Your subject line is one of the most important aspects of getting your email opened. Email marketing experts spend more time honing their subject line than all their other content combined!

For vacation rental owners, the idea for the subject line is to identify who we are and give a few words about our main story that invites curiosity. It is also important to not mislead. A "clickbait" subject line may get a lot of open clicks this time, but if your readers feel deceived they will unsubscribe or simply ignore future emails.

In the example box earlier in Chapter 23, the story was about some local birds visible from Sea Zen. "Sea Zen—introducing gannets, ballerinas and killers." The subject line gave the interesting contrasting character of the gannet birds without going over the top.

A soft subject line might be "Sea Zen—the gannets."

A clickbait subject line might be "Killings continue at Sea Zen," which might prompt plenty of opens this time, but readers will feel deceived and unsubscribe or dismiss your emails in future.

It turns out a subject line like "Sea Zen news—the birds are back" works well. It is interesting and helps the spam filters understand that this is a newsletter (good) and not some shady unsolicited email. A subject line like "Amazing super deal!!! Free night on us!!!" is likely to go straight to spam. Words like "free" and "deal" and repeated punctuation are red flags for the spam filters. Mailchimp has some good articles on how to avoid the spam filters. Long-term trust and interest are more important than a short-term win.

A/B testing

This is another way to check what is working best. The email software will allow you to set up two different versions of your email, send each to a sample of your list and allow you to decide on the best version before sending out to your full list.

For example, I wasn't sure in a certain month whether the subject line should feature my special offer or my lead story, so I ran an A/B test. It turned out the lead story did slightly better, so I ran with it. The fact that both versions were similar meant it didn't make much difference, so next time I agonized less and just went with my gut. The A/B test part is easy to use and well documented in Mailchimp.

When to send?

I found that I get more bookings when the sun is shining after a run of cloudy weather. After booking, one guest said, "Yes, I saw the sun shining and I decided we had to take some time off and get away from town!"

Armed with this information, I'll check the weather forecast for the next week and aim to send out my email newsletter at around the middle of the day on a sunny day in the middle of the week.

You can use your knowledge of your guests' behavior. You can also run tests and see what works best for you.

Another option is to send out emails a few months before the month the guests stayed previously. That way you can target annually recurring dates like birthdays and anniversaries. I have some guests who come the same date each year for their anniversary.

Length of newsletter

How long should your emails be?

Our attention spans are getting shorter and shorter. I like getting short emails with a link to more detail if I'm interested, so that is what I do with my newsletter emails. I also check with my readers, and they say that seems okay.

Frequency of emails

Yearly, quarterly, or monthly? I've experimented and found that a newsletter every one or two months works okay, and my readers agree. If you aren't sure, start quarterly and test with your readers.

Blast or value?

I feel squeamish when so-called experts talk about "email blasts." It conjures up an image of past guests being blasted with a fire hose. Hardly a way to treat guests.

I prefer to think of a polite offer of value that my guests will find useful and will hopefully result in a booking.

Using the newsletter recipient list to motivate your cleaner

Sometimes—rarely—guests leave a big mess in my rental. It drives my cleaner crazy, and she feels insulted that folks don't try to be tidy. We agree that I say nothing to those guests but prefer that they don't come back.

She gets great satisfaction when I confirm with her that the untidy guests have *not* been added to my email list.

Mobile-friendly newsletters

In 2018 over 75% of all emails were read on a mobile (McLeod 2018). Therefore, it's critical that your emails look good on a mobile.

Mailchimp has a "Design" option where you can have one font size for desktop viewing and a different size for mobile viewing. You can and should see how your email looks on both devices before you send it.

Most people don't realize that the default email view has images switched off. Most of your email readers will probably not bother turning images back on. So before you spend half an hour of your life tweaking that image to perfection, remember that most of your readers will not see it. Don't take it personally; it's just the reality of modern life.

Avoiding spam filters

Spam filters have a scoring system that applies to your incoming email newsletter. Things that the spam filters don't like are words like "free" and "bargain," multiple consecutive punctuation marks, email sourced from Gmail/Hotmail/Yahoo, etc. Your software system may rate your email before it is sent out. Mailchimp flatly refuses to send out emails originating from Gmail/Hotmail, etc. Mailchimp also has a rating to tell you if your email is close to triggering spam filters.

You might go as far as asking your guests to legitimize your address by sending an email to your address if they have not yet done so, e.g. if the booking is done behind the curtain via the online travel agency messaging system that keeps your email identity from your guests.

Overcome procrastination

Easy. If your target is for emails to go out every two months, schedule a reminder for the date to send out your newsletter, and act on it when your reminder comes up. You might get together with a buddy colleague and coach each other on meeting your email targets. It was the way members of our mastermind group got each other to deliver on a regular email schedule.

How do I get good topics for my newsletter?

You can set up a file to record ideas for your next newsletter and refer to it on the day your reminder says it's time to send out your newsletter. You can also store interesting newsy photos in the same file. You will be surprised how many helpful topic ideas you can get using this trick. You can also use unpublished ideas from last newsletter file.

You can also save ideas that relate to your theme. As an example, Japanese woodblock prints in a new exhibition triggered discussion of the original Japanese prints in Sea Zen. An easy and interesting story.

Examples of newsy topics

This can seem hard when you are starting out, but the world is full of newsy opportunities for your newsletter.

If your rental is in a regional holiday area, there's a multitude of ideas, including seasonally recurring events in nature and culture, as well as the food themes. If you are in a city, there are endless reviews to be done of your favorite places to visit, your favorite places to eat, new places opening, and more. If your rental has a theme, there are all sorts of stories that harmonize with it.

Regional vacation rentals	City vacation rentals
Seasonal • it's whale season again • it's breeding season for the koalas (/bowerbirds/king parrots ...) • truffle hunt time—and truffle dinner **Nature** • local bird series—the gannets (/wedge-tailed eagles/ bowerbirds/crimson rosellas ...) • local path closes due to landslip (/opens after landslip) • Our beach just ranked in top 10 in the country. **Our favorite/food** • our favorite café in the hills • our favorite drive in the forest • mulled wine for return guests in winter **Theme (Japanese Zen example)** • new Japanese robes for return guests • art exhibit has Japanese prints—like we do • try the spa—Japanese citrus style	**Seasonal** • it's football season (/baseball/ basketball/cricket ...) • It's film festival time (/comedy festival/arts festival ...) **Nature** • Our favorite park is Treasury Gardens (/Botanic Gardens ...) • we show visitors native animals up close at Healesville sanctuary (/city zoo ...) **Favorite food** • our favorite restaurant in Richmond, an oyster bar, around the corner • Der Raum bar nearby is in the world top 10 bars. **Culture** • new exhibition opening for Chinese entombed warriors (/French impressionists/ Japanese calligraphy ...) **Theme** • graffiti walk has same artist as our lounge wall

I wish I'd had the table above when I was starting up my newsletter!

Would you like monthly inspiration?

You can simply sign up to my example monthly Sea Zen newsletter. There is a sign-up link on the Seazen.com.au website.

Collecting images

So, it is time to send out your newsletter, and you have a great story but no images. What to do?

You can see if there is a legitimate image on Google Images. Did you know that you can find images that are legally okay to use? Once in Images, click the Tools option under the search box, then Usage rights, then Available for re-use. Then choose an image and make sure there are no restrictions on its use.

Alternatively, you can buy usage rights to an image using one of many stock photo websites, e.g. Istockphoto.com.

Or you can "collect in the moment," that is, be alert to story and photo opportunities in the background all the time, and every time you see an opportunity, snap. Put a copy in your "next newsletter" folder, record the idea in an "newsletter ideas" file. What you don't use next newsletter, you can hold over till the next. In no time, you will have a whole bunch of ideas and images.

For owners who enjoy social media, you can use the images and stories there too. I don't do that, having found social media to be a time-wasting distraction that gets far fewer bookings than the obvious main marketing sources like newsletters and loyalty schemes.

As mentioned earlier, few of your newsletter readers on mobile will actually view the images, so don't go to too much trouble over images. The more important thing to focus on is sending a regular newsletter. Actually sending a newsletter is more effective than procrastinating the sending of your newsletter via an excuse like "I'm still getting a few good images."

Using your newsletter topics to help your SEO

One way that your website is found on Google is where you have articles on your website that come up in long-tail search terms. For example, "wye river birds" is more likely to come up with my website if I have a number of articles relating to Wye river birds.

I typically write a post on the website relating to the newsletter topic. For example, I wrote an article on gannets as birds from Wye River, on my Seazen.com.au website. It is then more likely to be found by Google for "wye river birds." I can also start my email newsletter story about gannets with a few brief paragraphs, and for those who want to read more, there is a link in the email jumping to the website story (or Facebook post, etc.).

A different alternative—time-based reminders

One member of my mastermind group uses a different approach: he sends guests a series of reminders and news snippets based on the time since they stayed. He sends them automatically with an autoresponder one day after the stay, three days, three months, six months, nine months after the stay. It works for him. I prefer a simple newsletter to everyone.

Newsletter as a game changer

As I said earlier, after 20 years in the business I've learned that an email marketing newsletter has been the most effective at getting bookings. Also, it has zero cost other than time, and it results in direct bookings.

It is also a competitive advantage. Most owners are not prepared to overcome the mental challenge to implement a newsletter. That included me too in the early years of rental. Once you have started, you stand head and shoulders above your competitors.

Visit Holidayrentalmastery.com to see the latest tips and training courses about email newsletters.

> Key takeaway: a newsletter can be the most powerful source of repeat guests.

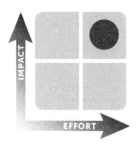

CHAPTER 26

Your Own Website—
Why You Need It

KEY POINTS

- Your website is where you can get many extra direct bookings from your loyalty scheme and online travel agency leakage.
- The current four website challenges are to be mobile-friendly, secure, flexible, and to meet changing Google guidelines.

Navigating

This chapter explains why you need it—how a website will help your vacation rental. It also explains some evolving challenges that your website will need to cope with.

The next chapter explains the approaches to getting a website to help you decide which one to take. The third chapter in the set explains the information your website should contain. If you've decided a website is just not for you right now, you can jump to Chapter 29.

Why have a website?

Your own website brings you extra bookings, direct bookings, flexibility, and control.

You can drive extra traffic from search, your newsletter and loyalty. Your own direct bookings save you commissions. Past guests can find you easily from your website. When referred guests hear about you, they can find your website directly. Guests from anywhere can find you from your SEO efforts. You can tell your own story and wow inquirers with your images, videos, and guest recommendations.

Without a website, you'll be dominated by online travel agencies

This is what your marketing system looks like *without* your own website. It is dominated by the online travel agency sites like Airbnb, Booking.com and Expedia. Your own bookings take a back seat, and your loyalty scheme struggles.

NO WEBSITE—OTAS DOMINATE BOOKINGS

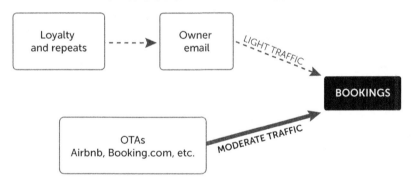

Your own website transforms your business

With your own website in place, all your loyalty referrals go straight to your own website. You can attract extra search traffic like Google My Business, Google Maps, Google organic search, your own SEO efforts, and local websites. You can also pay for ads to drive traffic to your website.

Traffic builds direct to you, and the online travel agencies have less of a share of bookings. You pay less commissions.

You are in control.

OWNER WEBSITE—STRONGER OWNER BOOKINGS

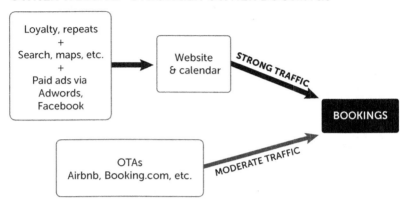

"Leakage"—searchers on online travel agencies will find your website

An indirect benefit of having your own website is that experienced searchers will find you on your OTA listing, then go off and find your own website, where they can get more information and often a lower price. This is sometimes called leakage.

Your prospective guests also like to have a conversation with you, something that most OTAs block.

OWNER WEBSITE—WITH OTA LEAKAGE

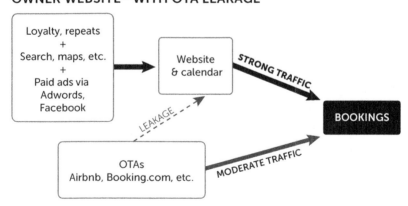

It is estimated that about 30% of browsers who find you on an OTA will leak to your own website, check you out, and often book direct. All of this reinforces why you do need your own website that can be easily found!

Evolving challenges

In the dynamic world of the internet, the current challenges are the trends to mobile-friendly, secure, and flexible sites.

Why you need a mobile-friendly website

Five years ago, most searchers used their desktop to search and to make the booking. That has changed, with most searchers using their mobile for their initial search. The majority are still making the booking on their laptop or tablet from a shortlist, but that also is trending toward mobile.

Google realizes this and penalizes sites in its search results that are not mobile-friendly or are slow to load on a mobile. The trend for good websites is to be flexible and visible on mobile, tablet and desktop. These sites are "mobile-responsive."

> Due to growing mobile search, websites should be "mobile-responsive" and visible to searchers on mobile, tablet and desktop. Google gives preference to mobile-responsive websites in its search results. Therefore, your website must be mobile-responsive.

What should your mobile-friendly website look like?

About five years ago, your desktop website needed to be visually attractive. Lots of images, lots of information, and all your questions answered. A cross between an informative brochure and a work of art. Owners succumbed to the temptation of having two or three columns with information crammed everywhere.

All of that has changed with mobile searching. Your website information should look good in a single column with vital information available without too much scrolling down. A big, fancy website can be incomprehensible on a mobile. Simplicity outperforms a fancy work of art.

> A simple single-column website outperforms a complicated website on mobile

Why security is important

> Hacking is a real risk. This happened to me—three times—in 2014. It prompts a sickening feeling deep in your gut. Twice some bad code was injected by some bad robots into my VR website code. Google "helpfully" added a note next to my website in its search results, something like, "Warning: this site may harm your computer." Another time, the site just stopped working.

At any moment, your website is being tested and probed by malicious robots from all over the planet. There are three new strains of malware created every second (Sundaresan 2018). If your security is weak, the robots will get in. You need to have backups in case the robots *do* get in. Good security today can be outdated security tomorrow. Ideally, you need to have an expert on hand or sound strategy to care for your website's security.

As you will see below, one of the big advantages of Wordpress. com is the extra security that you get by having restricted templates, widgets, and plug-ins. Just using the free WordPress version does not protect you, as you can have a multitude of insecure plug-ins, and a plug-in that is secure today can have a vulnerability that will make it insecure tomorrow.

> Your website needs to have very good security and regular backups

Your website needs to change with external requirements

As part of its aim to give users a better experience, Google periodically finds websites with practices that are not good for users. It usually penalizes these sites indirectly by dropping them lower in its search results but sometimes has explicit warnings like it does for sites with malware. Sometimes it removes the website from its search results entirely so your website becomes effectively invisible to searchers! In recent years Google has penalized sites that:

- are slow to load
- are not adaptive to mobile phones
- contain spam and deceptive practices
- contain duplicate content
- are http (less secure) rather than https (more secure)
- contain poor security parameters.

Mostly, these are minor and result in lower ranking by Google, but when it is important, your website will need to adapt. As mentioned above, when Google finds malicious code, it rightly throws the book at you.

> Your website will need to adapt to changing Google guidelines to be found high on Google

Key takeaway: your website is key to a lot of extra direct bookings.

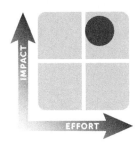

CHAPTER 27

Your Own Website— Choosing An Approach

> **KEY POINTS**
> - The four different approaches to building a website are described to help you make a choice: developer, package, free WordPress, hosted WordPress.
> - The most influential platform, WordPress, is explained.
> - Hosted WordPress on Wordpress.com is an attractive solution.

Choosing an approach

There are some fabulous website platforms out there, some very well supported systems, and some bare bones do-it-yourself systems. They can be expensive or low-cost. They can be set-and-forget or require a lot of ongoing work. Most importantly, there are various approaches that come with support to get you out of trouble with security and Google changes.

Your choice of approach needs to suit your budget and the degree of involvement you require. You will find a summary table after the next pages.

The four basic website approaches

1. Developer managed

You can engage a developer to build a website for you to your requirements. You need no IT skills. The developer looks after the building, the hosting, the maintaining, and the security. They can make edits to your website pages or they can give you tools to make the updates yourself. The sky is the limit in terms of the features they can create for you. Changing to another developer can be problematic. The more they do, the more it costs. Not cheap.

2. Vacation rental template package

Companies have designed standard templates for websites specifically for the needs of vacation rental owners. They help set your website up, they do the maintenance and look after the security. You can make changes to your website pages, but you are constrained to the standard templates they provide. A calendar is usually included. Sometimes the website can be integrated with add-ons like online booking engines. Examples are Lodgify, LiveRez. Specialist packages are well suited to owners or managers with multiple properties to manage.

Your website is not cheap, but someone else looks after all the technical worries; you just run your VR. A cheaper variation is to use a platform like Wix that hosts your website and has a template for vacation rentals. There are a number of these.

3. Owner controlled

If you have the interest and some basic IT skills, you can build the website yourself using free standard "content management systems," typically WordPress. You are in control and can create amazing websites that can do almost anything.

You can choose from thousands of website templates and 40,000+ plug-ins that provide special features and functionality. You provide your own hosting through a commercial hosting service.

It's not as hard as it seems, and there is lots of help on how to do it. Once you acquire the skills, you can develop any number of websites for virtually nothing.

COMPARISON OF APPROACHES

Developer Managed	VR Packages
• You engage a professional developer to build your website to your design • They look after everything.	• A company experienced in the VR industry provides you with VR website templates. • Examples are Lodgify, LiveRez.
Cost* • $500–$5,000 to build • $100–$500 p.a. to manage	**Cost** • Setup is usually free. • Lodgify $350 p.a. single site • LiveRez $3,500 p.a. multiples
Security • depends on developer skills, usually okay	**Security** • usually okay
Pros • A professional looks after everything. • Use any design you like. • Edit yourself or by your developer. • You need no skills, ever. **Cons** • Finding a good developer can be difficult. • You still need to specify the look and feel of your website. • Your developer may take a while to respond depending on their workload. • Mobile-responsiveness limited by developer skills.	**Pros** • You get a professional-looking website that works well for the VR industry. • You can have integrated features like online booking engines. • usually mobile-responsive. • Helpful for owners with multiple rental properties and for VR managers **Cons** • Your design is limited to the templates provided.
OVERALL • for owners who want minimum involvement • expensive	**OVERALL** • for owners happy with pre-set VR solution • moderately expense.

*Costs in US$ 2018, approx. only

Owner Controlled	Wordpress.com
• You use a package like WordPress to build your own website, located on your own hosting service. • You look after everything, supplemented by your own tech support.	• You use a standard template to set up your own VR website. • Automattic Inc. manages the hosting, security, backups, and Google requirements.
Cost • free software • hosting is $50–$200 p.a.	**Cost** • free setup • service costs <$100 p.a.
Security • can be a serious problem	**Security** • no problem
Pros • Wide choice of design features. • Lots of tech support available for market rates. **Cons** • You have to look after your own hosting, backups, and security. • You need to learn special technical skills. • Your website is exposed to security breaches and Google requirements, like mobile.	**Pros** • Considerable flexibility for design within 150+ templates provided, okay for VR websites. • Company looks after hosting, backups, security, and Google requirements. • responsive for mobiles. **Cons** • limited to supplied templates and about 20 plug-ins, which cover most VR needs. • need to rely on external calendar. • limited connectivity to services like Google Ads, FB.
OVERALL • for owners comfortable with IT challenges and risk • inexpensive.	**OVERALL** • for owners happy with moderate flexibility • inexpensive and secure.

The downside to owner controlled is you can be vulnerable to changing security and maintenance requirements. It is a good idea to have access to a tech support person who you can call on to help you with set up, security or maintenance problems.

Overall, the costs can be kept to a minimum, and the sky is the limit for look and feel and functionality.

Although WordPress is the dominant content management system used by DIY owners, you can choose from many others like Drupal, Joomla, Wix, etc.

4. Wordpress.com by Automattic

The Wordpress.com hosting service managed by Automattic Inc. is a particularly powerful alternative that I am very impressed by and that meets the needs of most VR owners, and the company looks after the technical issues like hosting, backups, security, and Google's requirements.

You control the look and feel within the constraints of 150+ template options. There are various training options, and if you want you can get some tech support to help you get started. Once set up, you can update your own webpages to your heart's content.

It is a very cost-effective approach, and I use it myself.

How each approach works

Website approach 1—developer managed

If you go down this path, you need to find a commercial developer with the right pricing, communications, and availability. The best way is to get a personal recommendation from someone you trust.

I once made the mistake of engaging a virtual assistant from the Philippines to build websites for me. It turned out his skills were exaggerated, it was hard for us to communicate clearly, and he didn't have his own security software or fast internet. I had some unpleasant security failures that we managed to patch up but found very stressful. We limped along through a few projects and parted company. It would have been better and faster to choose a local professional with good IT and communication skills.

To get a recommended website service, you might try networking with other VR owners or friends and family. The developer doesn't need to specialize in the vacation rental industry—any industry will do—but you do need to find someone you can trust at reasonable rates.

Do not make the mistake of getting a well-meaning family member or friend who is an IT whizz and has built a few websites. You require a long-term professional relationship with someone who is always going to be available and understands the changing needs of the industry, particularly security.

If all else fails, try searching for website developers on the internet, and make sure you can speak to other clients to make sure they are happy; however, this is potentially fraught, and a good personal recommendation from someone you trust is far, far safer.

One useful approach is to select two to five different developers though a service like Upwork.com and give them the same small task, and see how they respond with quality, speed, and communication. You select the best two and give them another more challenging task and then make the leap to choose one for your website project.

The result from using a developer depends on getting the right developer, a challenge in itself.

Website approach 2—using a vacation rental template package

If this is the way you choose to go, you can do a fair bit of research on the web to compare the different companies. You can also see some examples of the sites they have populated with client VR data. You may want to speak to some of their clients to see how they perform in practice, and you may find some other VR owners in your local tourism network who can share their recommendations.

Here are a few examples: Lodgify, LiveRez, Cloudbeds.

Lodgify is worth consideration at $29/mo. for one VR and $59/mo. for two to five VRs.

LiveRez is suited to owners with large numbers of properties and full business integrations like accounting. Monthly fees are around $280, and training alone can take six weeks. Overkill for small owners.

These websites are very useful if your business is growing fast and you want to add extra properties to one or more websites. They also have extra integrations with channel managers and various accounting software integrations.

For a small VR owner with just a few properties, the target readership of this book, these packages can be overkill.

Website approach 3—free, owner controlled

It sounds attractive—free software like WordPress that can be infinitely customized. The technical challenges of hosting and security mean you will need to get help or become an expert. Like the first approach, developer managed, you will need to find someone to provide support. Alternatively, you will need to train yourself to become an expert—not ideal if you want to spend most of your time building up your vacation rental!

I originally went down this path, but the security challenges meant I needed to pay for support, which was costly. *Be prepared for some distractions and costs with this approach.*

Website approach 4—hosted WordPress on Wordpress.com

This approach is cheap and secure, as the service includes hosting and security. The shift to mobile-friendly websites has driven the need for simpler sites with fewer features, for which Wordpress.com is ideal.

Currently, there is a small barrier in choosing the right template for a vacation rental website on Wordpress.com. Also, getting started can be confusing.

The industry is calling out for some simple training to help VR owners get started on Wordpress.com, and this approach will be a winner. I am confident that in coming months and years suitable training will emerge that will help this approach dominate the VR industry. Holidayrentalmastery.com will publicize suitable training when it emerges.

The prior two approaches generally use WordPress, so it's worth spending some time understanding more about it.

The WordPress juggernaut

It dominates the internet. Below are a few impressive statistics.

About 30% of the top 10 million websites on the internet in 2018 were powered by WordPress! It is used by global giants such as Sony, *The New York Times*, Volkswagen, Forbes and even the Facebook Blog. It powers about 21 million active websites, which collectively post 82 million posts per month, and it is steadily growing. It dominates content management websites at 60% market share, with Joomla the nearest competitor on 3% (Wikipedia 2018). The open-source WordPress was launched way back in 2003 by Matt Mullenweg, who launched Automattic, the commercial hosting service for Wordpress.com, a few years later.

My first website was based on the Joomla platform, but I found it very clunky. The story of how I changed to WordPress is interesting.

While using Joomla, I went to a Joomla workshop in Melbourne in February 2009, when the global Joomla gurus were in town. Was Joomla headed in the right direction? I hoped to make the global gurus aware from the user perspective of the clunkiness of the Joomla editor, which made it very hard to build webpages. Their response was, "Well, that is a minor issue; look at the sophisticated new database feature we have built." The Joomla folks were geeking out on the new feature but would always be blind to the fatal usability flaw in the very basics of their system.

Soon afterwards I changed to WordPress, which had all the easy user features I needed. There are over 40,000 plug-ins and thousands of themes to allow amazing customization. I went on to build a dozen websites on WordPress for my own use, and an equal number for others. I didn't realize it at the time, but I was part of a global surge to WordPress that has made it the dominant website platform on the planet.

In recent years I have been convinced that the version run by Automattic Inc. that hosts very secure websites on Wordpress.com is an amazingly inexpensive, safe, and powerful solution for VR owners.

The two different ways to use WordPress—free and hosted

The **free** version is open-source, available to anybody from a site called Wordpress.org. But there is a catch: you need to find your own hosting and support. The **hosted** service is available for a small annual fee from a site called Wordpress.com, run by Automattic.

Free WordPress	Hosted WordPress
• download from Wordpress.org free	• sign up to Wordpress.com, via Automattic Inc.
• arrange your own hosting	• annual fee <$100 gives you a hosted website
• infinitely customizable	
• security issues and complexity means pay for help or become an IT expert.	• limited but adequate features
	• secure and suited to VR owners.

SUMMARY OF WEBSITE OPTIONS

Developer website	VR packages
Someone else does the tech stuff, but can be costly.	Can be good for owners with 2-5 sites, e.g. Lodgify, Wix.
Free WordPress, owner controlled	**Hosted WordPress**
Risky, needs special skills or tech support.	Good for VR owners but needs a little effort to get started.

Currently, there is no cheap and easy solution for small VR owners. None of these are easy, but remember it may be worth $20,000 p.a. to your bottom line when combined with a loyalty system. The cost and effort will pay off, even with one of the more expensive alternatives.

In coming years hosted WordPress, i.e. Wordpress.com, may well become the go-to solution for VR owners. I already use it for several of my websites.

Check Holidayrentalmastery.com for our breakthrough training that takes VR owners through creation of a VR website on Wordpress.com, in easy steps.

> **Key takeaway: there are four viable options for building your website, with Wordpress.com an attractive solution.**

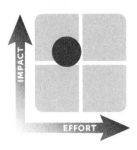

CHAPTER 28

Your Own Website—What's On It?

KEY POINTS

- The essential parts of a modern VR website are described.
- The home page is your opportunity to sell your brand.
- The imperative of mobile-friendly sites means your site needs to be simple, especially your home page.

The vital parts of a successful VR website

So, you have chosen a way to have your website built. What should it contain?

THE VITAL PARTS OF A SUCCESSFUL VR WEBSITE:

- a home page that says wow!
- a facilities page
- a bookings, rates, and calendar page
- an other rooms page (if you are selling different rooms or units)
- guest comments
- local guides
- news/blog
- about us

- a horizontal menu
- a single-column layout
- image galleries.

Your home page should say wow—economically

This is the page that guests will be looking at when deciding to book, and you have about two seconds to make that critical impression.

The most important part is your big, bright hero image—the one that says, "This is what this VR is all about" and sells your point of difference. Ideally, this should be part of an image gallery so the prospective guest can check other images without leaving the home page.

Now, while it would be nice to have all sorts of information on your home page, you must remember this page will mostly be viewed on mobile phones, and you need to keep it *brief*. It is a trade-off between selling and the attention span of a mobile user. Your home page needs a brief description that says what facilities you have and sells the emotional experience. Several paragraphs maximum.

You may choose to put your basic rates on the home page too, but always with a link to your calendar and online booking pages. If you can put your calendar on the home page, that is a bonus but not essential. It is helpful to serve up a recent review to credential you and a link to your page where there are more reviews.

In many ways, you have the same dilemma as the online travel agencies—what can you convey in a single page that conveys the essence of the vacation rental on offer? They have the same problem, and they have some clever layouts that you may get some ideas from. You have the luxury of unlimited space and pages.

In the footer you can list your name, address, and phone number to help credential your Google My Business listing.

Mobile-responsiveness imperative

While your home page has infinite flexibility, it also has to look good on a mobile—that means simple. No matter what you *could* put on your home page, it must be simple enough to be easily viewed on the small screen of a mobile.

Facilities page

List all your facilities. You might even have images or a gallery showing some of the more important facilities. An Airbnb researcher told me that some guests are "list blind" and don't register facilities on your list but lock onto images. Don't be shy to show images of the spa, the washing machine, the kitchen facilities, the fishing rod, etc.

Bookings, rates, and calendar page

Here you can describe your rates, extras, seasonal rates. You can show your calendar or, if it is managed externally, a link to your calendar.

Ideally, your guests should be able to book online, so show them how. Also, always invite them to contact you directly with your phone number. Email is problematic because of spambots, but I have always listed my email online and rely on spam filters.

Other rooms page

Where you separately rent different units or rooms, you can show images and descriptions of each.

Guest comments

Guests often validate their impressions by checking your reviews. You can post copies of current reviews from any of your sites including online travel agencies. I also like to insert some comments from my guest book, some of which are spectacularly insightful about your VR experience and sometimes are moving emotional experiences. Use them.

Local guides

Here you can post your own personalized guides to food, attractions, pet facilities, nature, etc. They credential you as a trusted local source, they help your guests, and they are a valuable source of search credibility for Google and SEO.

News/blog

Here you can write stories about the locality and local news. This can integrate nicely with your newsletter. The newsletter gives a quick paragraph; the blog has the bigger story. Each story is an SEO opportunity for Google to index you, particularly for the more unusual search terms. You can effectively market to your local niche that is invisible to the online travel agencies, e.g. local eating, birds, cycling trips, places for dogs to run, etc.

About us

You can tell your story, the personality for your VR. The start of a relationship with your guests.

Horizontal menu

A horizontal menu is economical for screen space. In the mobile view it may condense down to three small bars, enough in the mobile world.

> Key takeaway: the imperative of mobile-friendly sites means your site needs to be simple.

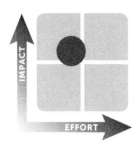

CHAPTER 29

Online Booking Capability

> **KEY POINTS**
> - An online booking facility on your website helps you get more bookings.
> - One popular booking facility is TheBookingButton, which passes guest information to you securely and can even process payments.

It really helps if guests can book directly online. Ten years ago, most guests preferred booking in person with an owner on the telephone. That has changed as people have become more comfortable buying online generally.

Now if someone calls to book directly with me, after asking a few questions, about half prefer to book online rather than pass details over the phone. No problem: the booking link is on the website.

Online booking also adds convenience for the guest. The guest can be searching at odd hours, find the website, and satisfy themselves that the experience is right—the photos look good and the reviews are reassuring. They check availability and price and book securely online on the spot. Job done. Easy. No need to find out if the owner is answering their phone or email; their holiday is booked.

For these reasons it's important to have a facility on your website for guests to book online. It will also save you a hefty commission.

> Online booking is good for guests and good for VR owners with their own websites

You have many options, but I chose TheBookingButton, from Site-Minder, which is a simple and powerful booking engine for small owners that can be accessed from a link on your own website. That link can be made to look like a button. There are other solutions, but they tend to work the same way.

How online booking sites work

You set up your rates and dates on their system with a few photos, and there is a public URL to your calendar with everything a guest needs to book. The link to that address goes wherever you want on your website. You can even make it look like a button.

Once the guest is ready to book, they click on the booking link and the booking engine takes over. The guest enters their dates, their details, and credit card securely. The details are stored on a secure server. The system instantly sends you, the VR owner, an email with details of your booking. You can log into the system to use the credit card manually, or payment can be taken automatically through a system such as PayPal and deposited into your account.

Price

There is a small monthly rental ($35/mo. in 2018) for TheBooking-Button, and no commission. When I had three VRs, I ran each as a separate room on the system with no extra price, excellent value.

Like all software, there are several competitors and some well below TheBookingButton's price but without the track record just yet. You should check the market periodically. This is another place where your mastermind colleagues may be able to help you.

Flexibility and control

When a guest books "instantly" using your online booking system, they book with you, under your control and your rules. You still retain the flexibility to unwind the booking by negotiating with your guest.

Conversely, the online travel agencies will penalize you savagely for declining a booking, e.g. loss of superhost status in Airbnb. Options like TheBookingButton give you power to act as you like. Obviously, you need to act responsibly to keep a good reputation.

Is TheBookingButton safe? SiteMinder claims to be the world's biggest online booking system with over $16 billion in revenue from thousands of hotels in 160 countries, and countless small VRs like you. It partners with some of the world's biggest accommodation websites like Booking.com and Ctrip. More information can be seen at www.siteminder.com/the-booking-button.

• • •

The other online booking options:
- Put a link on your website to your existing online travel agency listing—simple, but you lose control and are charged a commission.
- You can get various plug-ins that work with a WordPress site, with the various security headaches.
- You can get an integrated website/booking engine software from a number of providers, but deciding is not easy.
- Do nothing and lose online bookings.

I like the simplicity and cost-effectiveness of TheBookingButton, but you make up your own mind.

> **Key takeaway: an online booking facility on your website helps you get more bookings.**

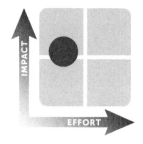

CHAPTER 30

Your Google "My Business" Listing

> **KEY POINTS**
> - Google gives you a *free* way to list near the top of its search results using My Business.
> - My Business is helpful for direct bookings to your website.
> - The listing process is simple but there is a delay in the process.

Did you know you can get to the top of Google for free, using a Google feature called "My Business"?

All vacation rental owners should be aware of Google My Business and how it works. It provides a box that comes up in the search results when you do a Google search like "accommodation wye river pet friendly." It gives about three featured businesses and usually an adjacent map showing the area. See next page.

Your My Business listing gives you a small page on Google with photos and a *direct link to your website*, your telephone number and email address, and a link to your availability on some listing sites. This is marketing gold!

MY BUSINESS LISTING ON GOOGLE SEARCH RESULTS

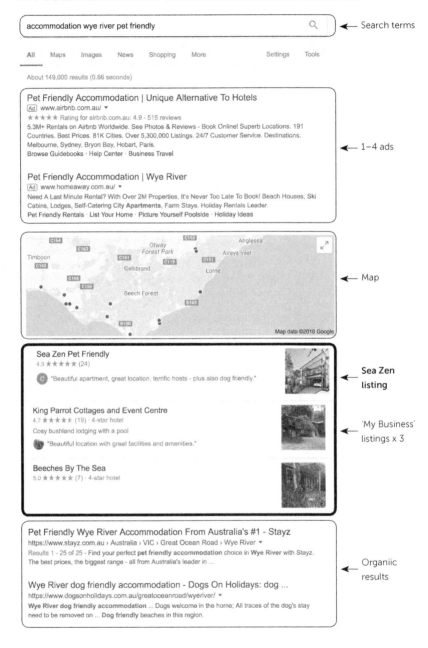

accommodation wye river pet friendly ⟵ Search terms

All   Maps   Images   News   Shopping   More   Settings   Tools

About 149,000 results (0.66 seconds)

Pet Friendly Accommodation | Unique Alternative To Hotels
[Ad] www.airbnb.com.au/ ▾
★ ★ ★ ★ ★ Rating for airbnb.com.au: 4.9 - 515 reviews
5.3M+ Rentals on Airbnb Worldwide. See Photos & Reviews - Book Online! Superb Locations. 191
Countries. Best Prices. 81K Cities. Over 5,300,000 Listings. 24/7 Customer Service. Destinations:
Melbourne, Sydney, Bryon Bay, Hobart, Paris.   ⟵ 1–4 ads
Browse Guidebooks · Help Center · Business Travel

Pet Friendly Accommodation | Wye River
[Ad] www.homeaway.com.au/ ▾
Need A Last Minute Rental? With Over 2M Properties, It's Never Too Late To Book! Beach Houses, Ski
Cabins, Lodges, Self-Catering City **Apartments**, Farm Stays. Holiday Rentals Leader.
Pet Friendly Rentals · List Your Home · Picture Yourself Poolside · Holiday Ideas

⟵ Map

Sea Zen Pet Friendly
4.9 ★ ★ ★ ★ ★ (24)   ⟵ **Sea Zen**
  © "Beautiful apartment, great location, terrific hosts - plus also dog friendly."   **listing**

King Parrot Cottages and Event Centre
4.7 ★ ★ ★ ★ ✦ (19) · 4-star hotel
Cosy bushland lodging with a pool   ⟵ 'My Business'
  "Beautiful location with great facilities and amenities."   listings x 3

Beeches By The Sea
5.0 ★ ★ ★ ★ ★ (7) · 4-star hotel

Pet Friendly Wye River Accommodation From Australia's #1 - Stayz
https://www.stayz.com.au › Australia › VIC › Great Ocean Road › Wye River ▾
Results 1 - 25 of 25 - Find your perfect **pet friendly accommodation** choice in **Wye River** with Stayz.   ⟵ Organiic
The best prices, the biggest range - all from Australia's leader in ...   results

Wye River dog friendly accommodation - Dogs On Holidays: dog ...
https://www.dogsonholidays.com.au/greatoceanroad/wyeriver/ ▾
Wye River dog friendly accommodation ... Dogs welcome in the home; All traces of the dog's stay
need to be removed on ... **Dog friendly** beaches in this region.

PROPERTY MY BUSINESS EXAMPLE

Sea Zen Pet Friendly — Link to website, Reviews, Address, Telephone, Map, Photos

Repeating—your vacation rental is also listed explicitly on Google Maps in the search results for the world to see. Nice!

Why Google wants you to set up your My Business account

Google's intent is to help searchers find some prominent examples for any business type they are searching for. Part of Google's aim is a better experience for its users.

Google is also playing a long game here. This direct connection with businesses positions it well if it chooses to become a competitor to the online travel agencies with its own travel portal.

My Business usually applies for all kinds of accommodation. It is also generic and works for all sorts of other businesses too. For example, if you search for "pizzas sandy beach" the search results will show three pizza businesses and where they are located. Also for plumbers, dentists, etc. You get the idea.

Google runs all sorts of experiments to try to find what searchers want most. At the time of writing, Google is showing three businesses. In the past it has been three, five, eight, and none, depending on what experiments Google is running at the time. The day you read this it may be different and different again the next. You need to go with the flow and seize your opportunity.

Google has also run experiments with its Google+ social feature, and the line between My Business and Google+ has been gray and still is. If you have an active Google+ account and a My Business listing, they are likely to reinforce each other.

Getting to the top of Google

As everyone knows, people click more on the higher search results because it's easier. If you want to get to the top of Google, you generally have three choices:

- You can pay for ads.
- You can get a My Business listing.
- You can try to rank at the top of everything else using SEO in the organic search results. As described in a separate chapter, this last choice can be difficult for many vacation rentals.

Clearly, a My Business listing mentioning your property near the top of Google results is extremely good value. It allows prospective guests three ways to book.

THREE WAYS GUESTS CAN BOOK VIA A MY BUSINESS LISTING:

- direct link to your website
- your telephone number
- link to availability dates on your listing on some listing sites like Booking.com

You also have the indirect but added value of your vacation rental name appearing in extra places, such as search and on Google Maps. It helps credential your name as an important brand in your area.

Quality of inquiries

I've found that the quality of some inquiries is variable. A searcher will often see your listing and immediately call the phone number without checking the details, e.g. if your VR is for families/couples—or even available. Calls may be for a stay a few hours or days ahead—not much value if you are a good marketer and booked weeks ahead.

That said, the smarter searchers will go to your website and check you out in more detail before calling. Also, you can have a conversation and strike up a relationship for a stay another time.

There is an argument that having a My Business listing will help you rank higher in the Google organic search results too.

Overall, it is mostly upsides to having a My Business listing.

Three steps for listing on My Business

1. Preferably, get your own website

It is not a requirement for My Business, but it's a big advantage to have your own unique website. This can be hard for some vacation rental owners, true, but it's not a problem for those who are dedicated to achieving rental mastery and high occupancy. It is also a handy barrier to the less motivated owners, and it allows you more prominence.

See Chapter 27 on getting a website—it's not as hard as some would have you think!

2. Ask Google for a My Business listing

You can do that here: www.google.com/business. You fill out several boxes, add a few photos, then submit for verification.

The category you choose for your business has been problematic in the past, sometimes vacation rental is an option and sometimes just hotel. Choose the closest to your operation; you can always change it later.

It is important to use the exact address, name and phone number used in your website for consistency. Google wants to see the one business described consistently everywhere. It will rank you higher for consistency.

3. Verification

Google takes registration *very* seriously, and the verification process in the past has had a time delay to ensure that your listing is stable. The usual method is for you to specify the address and follow the Mail option. This is not email, but the good old snail mail! Yes, Google goes to the trouble of sending a physical card through the post to your physical address to verify the business is where you claim it is! On the card is a code that you use to verify your business.

Even once verified, it can also take a while (usually one to four weeks) for your My Business listing to start appearing in the search results and on Google Maps. There are indications that Google is getting faster, but be prepared to be patient.

It's likely that if you already have an active Google+ account and are trusted by Google, the startup process will be much faster.

Other benefits

Barrier to competitors

There is a bit involved in getting listed, but nothing that getting organized and stepping through the sign-up process won't fix.

Many competing VR owners won't make the effort. All the better for you. If you make the small effort, you stand out from your competitors.

Reviews

Google wants reviews for your My Business listing, the more the better. Some commentators feel the volume and ratings are critical for you to rank high, and I'm inclined to agree.

Unlike many review systems, it can't be done anonymously: the reviewer's Google identity is posted. This puts off many reviewers, but it's just another barrier to entry that you can use to your advantage.

You simply need to ask your guests to post a review. You explain that it will help you. You give them the link, and over half will do a review for you. The initial few will grow, and you will stand out from your competitors.

You can take the link from the review page and test it. Once you have it, you email the invitation to your guest with a hotlink, saying "… to review just click here."

At one stage Google was scraping reviews from some online travel agencies or even using a direct feed from the OTAs. It isn't clear whether Google is still doing that.

Ranking higher on My Business

Clearly, even on My Business, it's in your interests to rank highly compared to other businesses.

> **THE KEY RANKING FACTORS ARE:**
> - consistency of the cluster of name, address, phone number on your listing and across the web. This is often referred to as NAP
> - complete information, including category, hours, photos
> - reviews and activity-like photos
> - prominence elsewhere on the web

To see the *latest* Google guidance, search for "google my business ranking." Google has several good answers, and dozens of private websites also provide useful information.

Connection to your online travel agency listing and calendar

In recent years, Google has made the connection between your listing on My Business and your listing on some OTA websites, like Booking.com, Expedia, etc. It makes it easy for searchers to check your rates and availability. The annoying downside is that a link to an OTA will cost you a commission, whereas a link to your own website can get you a booking without commission. You just hope searchers go directly to your own website.

Monthly reports

Google sends you a monthly report showing how many users saw your My Business listing, how many responded, and the trend on prior months. More gold!

Fit with other advanced marketing tactics

Your My Business listing fits nicely with other marketing tactics: connection to your website, visibility on Google Search, visibility on Google Maps, reinforcing your VR name, connection to Google Ads if you use it, reviews that guests may show their friends, direct phone inquiries to you.

It all fits nicely together, and it's free!

> **Key takeaway: Google My Business is helpful for direct bookings to your website.**

SECTION 3

TACTICAL ADVANTAGES

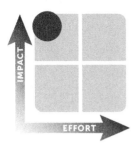

CHAPTER 31

Conversion Tactics

> **KEY POINTS**
> - Responding quickly to inquiries will often help make the booking.
> - Instant booking will give more bookings, but it must be appropriate for your style of VR.
> - Clear information for guests, a warm relationship, and good reviews help conversions.
> - You can usually convert gaps in your calendar by offering a bonus discount to extend the booking.
> - You can convert hagglers by demonstrating value.

You will find that advanced operators convert more inquiries to bookings than their competitors. This is no accident: they have honed their skills over many inquiries. Conversion is where the rubber hits the road, and it's the difference between beginners and mastery. The main tactics at a high level are **fast response, trust, relationship,** and **value.**

Fast response

To make the experience convenient for the searching guest, you need to respond quickly, have the facts easy to find, and make it easy to book.

When is fast response relevant?

For most online travel agency bookings, the OTA guest is usually committing to book with an offer that lasts 24 hours, so no rush.

However, sometimes they just make an inquiry, e.g. "Can my two cavoodle dogs come?" They are also likely to be making the same inquiry with other VR owners, so you need to get back fast and be the first to respond. It will be a masked communication via the OTA messaging system, so you can't actually talk with them. However, a fast response says you are professional and are likely to look after them.

When you have your own website, prospective guests have your email and telephone number, and often will call you direct—great. For email, they may be making the same inquiry to you and others, so a quick response will put you ahead of your competition. Again, it will show you're professional.

> I explained to a friend, Julie, who was struggling with conversions, that a quick response is critical.
>
> "Oh, but I do respond quickly," she said. "I jot down the inquiries as they come in and always respond later that night when I've finished my day, always within eight hours."
>
> I explained that quick means eight minutes, not eight hours. By the time she had responded, the inquiries had gone cold and she converted few of them.

There are a few tips to responding quickly. You can switch on a text alert if available on the online travel agency booking platform. You can also set up sound alerts in your phone for when an inquiry comes in.

You can also explain to family that part of your business is fast response. You can check that they do not mind, and then at a later date you can disappear without embarrassment for a few minutes while you make the call—and take the booking. I've even stopped on a freeway turnout to make the call and get the booking!

I like to contact the guest promptly, if I can, and simply say, "This is our courtesy call we give everyone inquiring, just in case I can answer any questions." Searchers often respond positively. "Wow that was fast, thank you so much, how can I book?"

If I ask them how they found us, there is a typical response: "I really don't know. A few hours ago I started searching on the internet and I'm a bit confused. It's a relief to talk to someone and just make the booking."

Where the inquiry is unresolved, you should have a follow-up system to remind you a few days later and send them an email: " … Just checking if you are still interested in booking." Gmail Boomerang is a great system for follow-ups to put the target email in the top of your inbox at the time you specify, e.g. a few days later.

Instant booking

In the current online travel agency world, the OTAs also want to make it fast and convenient, and they promote "instant booking," where the guest books the moment they make a committed booking inquiry. The OTA gives you higher ranking in their algorithms when instant book is turned on, and you get more inquiries.

For some owners, like me, who can greet and monitor the guests onsite and where the group is just a couple, you can control the risk and an instant booking is okay.

For VR owners with remote large houses that can be used for parties, the risk is higher and the owner's stresses are much higher. Pre-screening can be critical before agreeing to a booking and even then, it can be hard to screen using just the online travel agency messaging system. For that reason, owners of those larger and remote houses would be wiser to turn instant book off.

Trust

The searching guest may not be comfortable initially that what you are offering matches the reality. It isn't personal; they have learned the hard way that some advertising is misleading.

This is easily resolved. On your listing you should have some glowing reviews from guests who have enjoyed their stay with you. You should also have lots of photos on your website listing, about 20+, so they can see what it is that they are getting and you can put their fears at rest.

When I ask guests after they booked why they chose us, they often say, "I loved the photos and your reviews are great." You are also tapping into social proof, covered Chapter 33. If you can do that bit extra—lots of photos and reviews—it is a bit more effort initially, but it puts you ahead of your competitors. You've just overcome another barrier to business.

Given the blocks that online travel agencies put between you and your prospective guest before the booking, having your own website allows smart searchers to check out your site, get your details, and have the conversation with you if they wish. Another argument for your own website.

It goes without saying that your calendar and rates should be up-to-date so the guest already knows your availability and rates at the time of the inquiry, and whether there are any hidden costs.

I also like to say, "Our price is the price—no hidden extras, no surprises."

Relationship

"Relationship sells." As a hard-nosed engineer, when I first heard this quote years ago from a former vice-president of marketing from HP, it didn't make sense. Why should someone buy something just because they know them, when the facts speak for themselves?

Now older and wiser, I've learned more about the psychology of persuasion, and indeed as humans are complex, a relationship is very powerful. As explained in Chapter 20: Psychology, if you get to know someone and help them, there is a powerful sense of obligation on their part that will usually result in them buying. In the VR world, they make the booking.

If you can have a conversation on the phone with your undecided guest and help them and strike up a rapport, you are well on the way to a sale.

Some amazing VR owners go a step further and promptly send the inquirer a link to a personalized video lasting about 30 seconds, in which the VR owner addresses the inquirer by name and gives a brief introduction with an invitation to talk further. I gather it works really well in markets where guests stay for long periods. If nothing else, it gets attention and helps stand out from the crowd. Try it after you master the basics.

Value

From benchmarking against competitors, your prices should give your guests good value but not necessarily be low, because discerning guests with a flexible budget want an excellent experience that they are prepared to pay for.

How can you assure them of an excellent experience? Your reviews are important evidence that other guests have enjoyed their experience at the price. If they feel ripped off, guests won't leave a review, and intuitively inquiring guests know that good reviews are at least evidence of good value, particularly if the review has the phrase, "We'll be back."

As explained in the Customer Obsession chapter earlier, after feedback from my cleaner I realized we provide a lot of extras that our competitors don't, so I made a list: "The amazing 35 extras you get for free at Sea Zen." You can still find the download on Seazen. com.au.

That is another tool for helping guests understand the value they will get if they book. If an inquirer is unsure if they will come,

I'll send them the list of 35 extras and a recent glowing review, with an invitation to call if I can help them with any questions about the area. They usually book.

Other tactics—converting gaps between bookings

You will often find that you are left with a gap of a day between bookings. Maybe at the start or the end, or maybe the start and the end. For folks like me, single-night bookings are high overheads for cleaning and attention with a low margin. So, what to do?

You can offer the most recent guest an extra night at a discount. I have found by experiment in my market that two out of three take up the offer for a 50% discount for the extra night, and I have a time limit of 24 hours for the offer to force a decision (psychology's scarcity principle). The guest is happy, and you get a good margin for the extra night that would ordinarily be vacant.

If the first guest doesn't take up the offer, you can make the offer to the guest on the other side of the gap.

Where there is a gap at the start and the end of the most recent booking, you will lose two nights' income. The obvious action is to check if the guest has flexibility to shift forward or back a night, freeing a two-day gap that you can sell. By experiment in my market, I've found that guests are flexible about half the time, particularly if you have struck up a rapport during the booking process and you ask quickly after the booking—before they lock in their plans.

Haggling

In some cultures it is expected that the purchaser haggles for a discount. "Your price is too high!" It is not a criticism of value; it's just what some people are conditioned to do, and sometimes it works, so why not?

In the early days I was offended by a request for a discount, as I interpreted it as a personal criticism of my fabulous VR experience on offer. Foolishly, I would be defensive, or fume for days at what I saw as an insult, making me far less productive than usual. My loss.

Later I realized it wasn't personal, it was just a routine that some folks follow. There are ways of answering a request for a discount that keep everyone happy.

These days I just say, "I'm sorry, we don't discount as our price is fair and one reason we are the most booked property in our area, and our guests are happy, as you can see from our reviews. If you have a limited budget, could I suggest you try several other properties in the area like [name 1] and [name 2]. While you are thinking about it, could I send you our list of 35 things you get for free with us that you don't get with competitors?"

They can see I provide value at my price point, and if they do have a genuine budget limit, I have helped them out. The moment the call is ended, my mind is untroubled, and I can move on to other things.

By experiment in my market, I have found that about two-thirds will go ahead and book.

> **Key takeaway: you can usually convert gaps in your calendar by offering a bonus discount to extend the booking.**

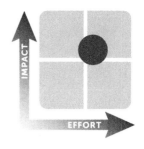

CHAPTER 32

Last-minute Levers To Pull

KEY POINTS

- You can increase occupancy by having some last-minute tactics to get late bookings.
- The most effective tactic is to have your own list of past guests who want to receive last-minute specials.
- Other tactics include discounting, Google ads, and Facebook ads.

Let's say you are usually fully booked, but there are a straggling few days vacant in your calendar in the coming week, and on the top of that you have a cancellation. You may be facing five days unbooked in the coming weeks, but you know you rarely get last-minute bookings. What can you do? All is not lost. There are several levers you can pull. In order of effectiveness:

- last-minute list
- discounting
- Google Ads
- Facebook
- website.

Exclusive last-minute email list

You can have a list of past guests who want last-minute specials. Let's say you have a regular email newsletter going out to past guests; in the newsletter you can invite guests to join your exclusive last-minute list for last-minute vacancies and cancellations. You may get 5% of your main list to sign up to your last-minute list, which can be enough to sell those last straggling bookings.

Using an automated email system like Mailchimp, it takes just 10 minutes to send out an invitation to book those last days at a discount. It usually works for me.

Sending last-minute specials to your entire list would be intrusive to your list, resulting in mass unsubscribes and socializing the entire list to wait for special discounts before booking.

Discounting

You can simply discount the rates for the last-minute dates in your main calendars.

Google Ads

You can have some special discount ads set up in Google Ads and just switch them on for a few days.

Facebook

You can run some pre-set Facebook ads, or if you have a group of Facebook followers, you can put out the special to the group.

Website

Some colleagues found past guests often looked at their VR website, so they simply posted cancellation specials on the home page. After a few years, folks started looking at the home page for specials.

> **Key takeaway: the most effective tactic for last-minute bookings is to have your own list of past guests who want to receive last-minute specials.**

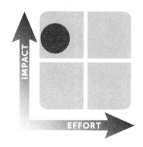

CHAPTER 33

Guest Reviews

> **KEY POINTS**
> - Reviews are the critical social proof of your VR value.
> - You can increase the review response rate by how you ask for reviews.
> - Negative reviews can be turned around in your favor.
> - Reviews on Google My Business can help direct bookings and SEO.

In the chapter on the psychology of influence, I showed that we are irrationally influenced by the behavior of others around us via social proof. Reviews are the ultimate social proof, the measure of trust. They tell everyone that your VR is what you claim it to be and they can safely book with you. It is consistent with the research statistic that 70% of consumers worldwide trust other consumer opinions online, a much higher proportion than those who trust a company's claims (Nielsen 2009).

Many guests say they only book after checking the reviews for a property. So you as an owner have to treat reviews seriously and have them work for you.

> "I liked your photos, but I only booked after checking the reviews"

You need to have a steady trickle of reviews over as long a period as possible, preferably one or more a month. I sometimes shake my head when I see a beautiful, well-run VR with just a few reviews, showing that the operators don't understand the industry, and they are probably losing many potential bookings.

Can you influence the number of reviews?

Yes! Sadly, some VR operators say that they can't influence the number of reviews, but nothing is further from the truth.

> In a former corporate role measuring customer feedback for internal services for 40,000 staff, I measured response rates. When customers were given a general invitation to provide a review, only 2% responded. But when they were sent a personalized invitation to review a specific recent event, the response skyrocketed to 40% and sometimes to 60%. I have found the same principle applies for VR guests.

The key point here is that the frequency of response depends almost totally on *how* the customer is asked. The online travel agencies routinely ask guests to review their experience with a modest response, but when *you* ask, the response rate skyrockets.

In a previous chapter (16: A great guest experience) we saw that there are many customer touchpoints that you can use to understand the customer experience and to help build a relationship. If you do that well, you can have any number of reviews and good ratings. Of course, this assumes you are creating a genuinely positive guest experience.

> To get more reviews, you must ask!

While that sounds obvious, asking a relative stranger for something can be hard for some folks, and it was for me too initially. It is another of those wonderful barriers to mastery. Once you get through it, you will be ahead of your competitors.

A friend told me how he does it. "Monday is my reviews day. I have a template and send out a request to the guests who have stayed in the last week. But not those who complain."

Here is my formula:

1. Make every opportunity to get to know your guest and build some kind of relationship.
2. If you can contact them at the end of their stay, explain your small business is dependent on reviews and ask if it's okay to send them a review.
3. Check for any comments in the guest book and the onsite feedback sheet, often these are very helpful and gracious comments.
4. Check how clean the guests left the property.
5. Call and send an email to the guest, making a connection to their stay with a link to where they can leave a review. (Nice meeting you, thank you for your comments on the feedback sheet/thank you for leaving the place so clean/no problem about the broken glass, etc.).
6. Just do it every week!

The most important part is the "just do it" part! Steps two, three and four can be done remotely if you are creative and you have good communication with your cleaner, who can text you a photo of the feedback sheet and the guest comment.

Do you ask everyone for a review?

No. Your competitors don't ask clearly unhappy guests, and nor should you.

Anyone unhappy has the option to complete a review, and they will if they feel strongly about it. What can you do about unhappy folks? If you pick up a vibe that leaving guests are unhappy, such as negative comments from the feedback sheet left behind, immediately call them, thank them for their frankness, and explain what you will do about the issue. Most folks want to be respected and acknowledged, and early comment will prevent negative public reviews much of the time.

Target review frequency

A good rule of thumb is to have at least one review per month per platform to establish a steady and long-term reputation of dependability.

Handling negative reviews

We are all human. Sometimes folks have a bad few days at work, and you cop the brunt of it in a bad review. It can be hurtful and seem unfair when you are pulling out all stops and the guest is picky over all sorts of minor things. However, the guest's perception is the guest's reality, and you are unlikely to change it.

How you react matters. If you can respond to a problem onsite before a review, you have a good chance to retrieve the situation. One golden rule is to react how you would if the roles were reversed and you were the unhappy guest.

At one stay, the stair lights were switched off without my cleaner noticing, and an older guest who was recovering from a medical condition tripped and fell. Luckily, no serious harm was done, and they told me while they were staying. I was mortified, thinking What would I want if it happened to my partner? I apologized profusely, ensured that the lights were rectified permanently, and gave them a credit for the full stay. They didn't give a negative review, they loved the return visit, and they were even grateful!

Another approach is to ask what they would like you to do. All these situations are an opportunity!

In all review systems I know, you can respond. Remember, you are on show to the public, and everyone realizes that sometimes guests can be unreasonably unhappy. Firstly, don't respond when you are emotional over the review. Take your time and view this as an opportunity to be genuine and positive in public.

Next, thank them for taking time to give their opinion, and as appropriate say you are sorry that they feel that way. Then acknowledge the concerns raised in the review, and if you are going to change something, say so. If your response appears positive to an impartial observer, you have done your job and may even have left a very good impression overall.

Review: 6/10

"Cooking facilities were average … Bed was average and not comfortable for us …"

My response:

"Hi [name], thank you for your feedback on the kitchen, we will upgrade the pots and pans … Beds can be personal; we purchased a top-quality bed and three prior reviews on this site alone have singled out the bed for comfort—"very comfortable," "extra comfy," and "unbelievable"; sorry it was not to your liking. Thank you for your frank feedback. We are constantly striving to give our guests the best experience, which is why we are the most booked property in Wye River."

Reviews as a weapon

Sometimes, unreasonable guests may threaten to leave a negative review over a small incident unless you give them a full refund. This is tricky, and if they are clearly being unreasonable, you can contact the online travel agency where the review will be made, foreshadowing the problem and asking for their support. In some cases, competitors have left false reviews to damage reputations, and have been prosecuted by consumer agencies and even jailed (!), but this is unlikely to happen without a huge distraction to your business. Best by far to respond to problems onsite reasonably and respond to reviews positively, even if the guests are picky.

Airbnb reviews—learn from them

No one does reviews better than Airbnb. In their early years they listened to their host owners, who wanted a way to understand the risk they were taking with guests, in just the same way that guests used reviews to understand the risk they were taking staying with hosts.

So the reciprocal review system used by Airbnb was born. The guest reviews the host and the host reviews the guest, both done blind before the other's review is published. The parts that will be public are clear to the reviewer, and the reviewer is invited to make private comments to share with the other. Both sides have a common interest in leaving respectful reviews, and the review participation rate is extremely high. Recently, a scraper site (Insideairbnb. com) found that there were three reviews per month per active listing in Melbourne.

Given that guests also have some skin in the game, they realize that if they mistreat the property they can be publicly exposed. I have found that Airbnb guests rarely mistreat our properties. The Airbnb review system is one of the reasons for its popularity, giving Airbnb 100% compound annual growth in the early years.

Guest reviews are one of the factors used by Airbnb for ranking listings. How much impact? That's not known exactly, but clearly, the more good reviews, the better for your ranking.

Google My Business reviews—they are worth the effort

There may be value in inviting your guests to make a review on Google My Business, given the strategic position that many, including myself, consider that Google My Business/Maps will occupy, and given that reviews are a ranking factor for it. The system requires the reviewer to post their Google account name publicly; however, I have found that over half of guests asked to post on Google My Business will do so.

An advantage of Google My Business is that it feeds directly into the Google+ system, which adds to your SEO. Time will tell if it pays off. I think it will, and it may even translate into a handy SEO advantage in itself.

When asking for reviews for an online travel agency booking, should you ask for the OTA review, Google My Business review, or leave it to the guest? If your OTA reviews are sparse, you might choose the OTA. Just choose one and send your guest the hotlink by email. Make it specific and easy.

Reviews are a challenge for VR owners. Doing reviews well will give you another advantage over your competitors.

Key takeaway: reviews are the critical social proof of your VR value.

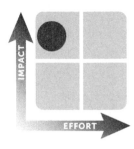

CHAPTER 34

Understanding And Exploiting The Big Four

> **KEY POINTS**
> - The four main online travel agencies are Airbnb, HomeAway/VRBO, Booking.com, and TripAdvisor.
> - This chapter explains the differences between the online travel agencies and provides a comparison table.

Airbnb vs HomeAway vs Booking.com vs TripAdvisor

In Chapter 4, I showed how Airbnb has dominated growth in the vacation rental industry.

However, there are another three major online travel agency listing sites that are very important for getting bookings for your vacation rental property. Here are the big four:

- Airbnb
- HomeAway/VRBO
- Booking.com
- TripAdvisor.

In this chapter you will see how these big four "gorillas" compare, and how you as a small VR owner can use them to your advantage.

Airbnb

The market darling, Airbnb, has made it extremely easy for you to list your property and manage it. It continues to grow exponentially and in 2018 has around 5 million listings of which most are individual properties with their own personality. Most properties have been in urban areas, with lower prices, but this is changing as more traditional vacation rental owners are jumping on board.

The business model is to charge the owner a modest 3%–5% commission, and to charge guests a separate 5%–13% booking fee. The company looks after all payments and pays you the net revenue soon after the guest stays.

Airbnb changed the industry by allowing the owner to rate past guests, building up some reputation history about guests. So for new booking inquiries, the owner can make a more informed judgment about the guest, even though the guest and owner are restricted to email until the booking is made.

Risk is also reduced by $1 million of damage insurance, which comes with fine print. Like HomeAway and TripAdvisor, a security deposit can be handled through the system.

Airbnb has a subtle mix of incentives and penalties to encourage "desirable" owner behavior. This includes allowing instant booking by guests, avoiding cancellations, and having good guest reviews. Compliant owners are rewarded by higher rankings and more bookings.

Airbnb's foundation story of allowing room sharing in the sharing economy captivated journalists, who gushed about the new company and helped drive awareness and viral growth, a bonanza for the founders. The current reality is most listings are for entire apartments and houses, and the company is aggressively moving on luxury rentals, China, business travelers, and even hotels!

The former lines that were drawn around the sharing economy are now blurring, and almost any accommodation is on offer. This blurring extends to all the online travel agencies as they push to add more listings.

The ongoing exponential growth in supply of listings has led to growing pains, local bans for short-term rentals and a flood of competition into your market.

HomeAway/VRBO

This company has long specialized in vacation rentals, growing by acquisitions until it too was acquired, by the huge Expedia agglomerate. It had around 2 million global listings in mid-2018. It is growing steadily, but at a lower rate than Airbnb.

HomeAway has specialized in larger houses suited to family holidays, but that is changing to smaller properties as the market expands. It has many customer-facing sites such as VRBO and previously Stayz.

Initially disdainful of Airbnb as an upstart targeting millennials in small apartments, HomeAway found itself with an outdated model and has now copied almost all of Airbnb's business model. It now has similar-level fees for owner commissions and guest bookings and has an owner review system of past guests.

Its software is clunkier than Airbnb's, but as you would expect of an Expedia unit, it is innovating fast. It has planned to pass on much of the initial deposit moneys when paid (not yet in 2018), whereas Airbnb keeps all your money until the stay.

Like Airbnb, the owner–guest relationship is limited to email until after the booking is made, and as the model changed that has caused much angst with owners, who preferred the relationship and informed choice they had in the prior model.

Booking.com

This giant has specialized in renting rooms *for hotels* all over the world. It has been very successful in its market and in recent years has aggressively targeted growth in vacation rental listings. In sheer market size and net revenue, it outperforms the other three gorillas, but it has only recently become an important option for VR owners as a source of vacation rental bookings. It claims around 5 million "alternative" *room* listings in 2018, and 27 million when including hotels. It has several affiliated sites in Asia, like Agoda and Ctrip.

The business model is different from the other three, in that its offering is centered around pleasing guests who can instantly book from a wide choice of accommodation. It has also offered guests easy cancellation. The rental owner collects all money, retrospectively paying a 12%–15% commission to Booking.com. Unlike the other models, there is no information about the guests until after they book.

The model works well for small hotels, where there is someone onsite to manage risk as they greet, screen, and monitor guests. Also, multiple rooms give the hotel owner the ability to over-book and manage a constant trickle of cancellations.

For vacation rental owners the Booking.com model has its challenges, the main one being assessing risky guests who will usually stay in a remote location unsupervised. There is no information about the guest, no reviews of the guests, and no ability to refuse a booking without a ranking penalty. A late cancellation will often mean 100% loss of a booking for a VR owner. However, if you look deep into the options you can specify a stricter cancellation policy and collect money within 42 days of the stay.

Guest damage is seen by Booking.com as an owner insurance problem, whereas VR owners like to manage risk. Stories are emerging, like Airbnb, of extensive damage to Booking.com vacation rentals from house parties. Unlike Airbnb, Booking.com offers no backup insurance for such events.

In many countries, Booking.com uses its market dominance to insist on owners agreeing to its "lowest price guarantee," whereby the owner is not allowed to offer anywhere on the internet a lower price than the price listed on Booking.com. This effectively blocks direct bookings. In some countries, the price-fixing arrangement has been seen as anti-competitive, and Booking.com, due to its market dominance, has been forced to wind back these practices. In other countries owners mitigate the price-fixing by offering discounts for loyalty. Some VR industry leaders have labeled Booking.

com as arrogant toward VR owners. Even the language on the website backend refers to "your hotel."

Unlike with the other three online travel agencies, the owner submits their listing information, and the company decides the wording of the site listing to fit with their guidelines. With the other OTAs, the owner can make up their own wording.

So why would a VR owner like yourself choose to list with Booking.com with all these restrictions? Many don't! Owners with an onsite presence can manage risk. Other owners have used Booking.com themselves overseas extensively, and there is a realization that Booking.com has great brand strength. The attraction of another good source of bookings is often enough for owners to sign up. I have used Booking.com without problem, with a steady trickle of bookings.

TripAdvisor

TripAdvisor is a clear market leader in terms of site visits by travelers, who look to its extensive database of reviews for travel advice while checking out a destination or accommodation provider.

However, TripAdvisor has a particularly low conversion rate for bookings as a fraction of site visits. In the past it has been hard for travelers to find vacation rental listings, but that too is changing as TripAdvisor chases growth in the vacation rental industry. Given the large volume of site visits, for some markets TripAdvisor is a good source of bookings. Just to confuse things a little, vacation rentals are managed through FlipKey, a TripAdvisor subsidiary, and listed on various websites including TripAdvisor itself.

Like HomeAway, TripAdvisor/FlipKey has chosen to copy the Airbnb business model with a similar commission and booking fee structure, and similar processes for bookings, payments, and reviews. Payments are received the day after the guest arrives.

Some reports from my colleagues show fewer bookings via TripAdvisor than from other online travel agencies.

COMPARISON OF ONLINE TRAVEL AGENCIES (AS AT 2018)

Aspect	Airbnb	HomeAway/ VRBO	Booking. com	TripAdvisor/ FlipKey
VR listings globally	5 million	2 million	5 million	1 million approx.
Commission payable	3%–5%	5%–7%	12%–15%	3%
Guest booking fee	Typically 11%	Typically 11%	Nil	Typically 11%
Instant booking	Optional	Optional	All bookings	Optional
Reviews of guest by owner?	Yes	Yes	No	Yes
Reviews by guest?	Yes	Yes	Yes	Yes
Payments timing	After check-in	After check-in	By owner	After check-in
Payments handled by	OTA	OTA	Owner	OTA
Security deposit	Optional	Optional	Owner handles	Optional
Conversation with guest prior to booking	Via site email	Via site email	None	Via site email
Information for assessment of guest risk	Good info	Partial info	No info	Partial info
Overall suitability for VRs	Market leader	2nd market leader	Can expose to risk	Performance unclear

In the past there have been instances where policy changes have led to review history being lost for many listings. Due to this and other events, many in the VR industry have less confidence in TripAdvisor than in its competitors.

Exploiting the online travel agencies

1. Make "leakage" to your own website easy

As many as 30% of guests are wary of higher online travel agency costs and will try to research your own website before booking, after looking at OTAs. If they find you, they will book direct.

You need a clear property name in your OTA listing, and that should match the name of your website, so guests wanting to book direct on your website can find you easily and book.

2. Choose the right online travel agencies for your local market

Airbnb and HomeAway usually dominate the vacation rental industry in terms of ease of use and availability in most markets. I recommend owners use both. You can experiment with others, but as mentioned in Chapter 8, I always suggest you network with your fellow owners in your area to share information about which OTAs are working well or not *in your market*. A five-minute conversation with a few colleagues can be as useful as a 12-month trial and can save a lot of time and effort.

A good choice will deliver you more bookings. But remember all the big OTAs have serious commissions. Your longer-term goal should be to **build up direct bookings** through repeat bookings and your own website.

3. The best match problem

Online travel agencies help inquiring guests by "best match," i.e. only showing properties available for dates selected by the inquiring guest. This means if you have a large minimum number of nights stay, your VR will be displayed less than VRs with a smaller minimum. You should take that into account when deciding your minimum number of nights stay.

4. Optimize your use of each online travel agency to rank higher

Each OTA has its own reward algorithm for rewarding better-performing hosts with a higher ranking and more bookings.

The next sections help you optimize your listings for each of the larger online travel agencies—Airbnb, HomeAway, Booking.com and TripAdvisor.

> **Key takeaway: Airbnb, HomeAway, and TripAdvisor have similar models; Booking.com is more guest-centric.**

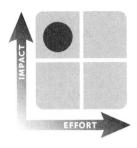

CHAPTER 35

Optimizing For Airbnb

> **KEY POINTS**
> - Be prepared to capitalize on an early boost in the first weeks of listing.
> - Qualifying as an Airbnb superhost will mean you are doing well with most factors in the Airbnb ranking system.
> - Instant book gives you an advantage in ranking but comes with operational risks.
> - Include your VR name in your title to maximize leakage via direct bookings to your website.
> - It is important that your VR stands out in the listings and is not just another cut-price Airbnb commodity.
> - Keep tuned for Airbnb innovations and exploit them ahead of your competitors.

How do you get listed higher in the Airbnb search results? Airbnb doesn't publish its ranking algorithm, but in general it rewards hosts who do the kinds of things guests appreciate. Mostly, it's common sense.

Guests appreciate things like good reviews, accurate description, cleanliness, accurate calendar, up-to-date information, quickness to respond, no cancellations, ability to book instantly, hosts who accept most bookings, ability to stay one night, easy cancellation, ability to stay with a superhost.

Flipping this around gives the kinds of behaviors that get hosts rewarded by a higher search listing.

Good reviews

The average host review score is 4.5 out of 5. You need to get a consistently high review score. To do that you need to give your guests a good experience.

Accurate description

Guests are asked in reviews if the experience matched the description. If not, you will be marked down.

Cleanliness

Airbnb knows that guests rate cleanliness as essential. You need to get five out of five for cleanliness in ratings.

Up-to-date information

Every 30 days, Airbnb checks to see that you are logging on and updating your calendar. It even likes changes to description, updates to photos, etc.

Quickness to respond

You need to respond to messages within 24 hours. Earlier, on average, is better.

No cancellations

If you cancel, you will be penalized. Airbnb understands that guests hate cancellations by hosts.

Instant booking

Turning instant book on will help you rank higher by the algorithm. Guests can also choose to only look at listings that have instant book on, so this is a double weighting.

Acceptance of bookings

Airbnb expects you to accept bookings, with one exception. You can reject bookings that you are uncomfortable with if something in their guest profile or comments leads you to believe they will not keep to house rules. To reject others will mark you down.

Short stays

If you accept one-night bookings, you will get more bookings, as some guests will want them.

Easy cancellation policy

Some guests will give preference to listings with easier cancellation policy.

Superhosts

Guests can choose a filter to narrow searches to superhosts, so superhosts get an advantage with extra bookings, as well as a boost through the Airbnb algorithm. Airbnb say superhosts earn 22% more than other hosts. Around 20% of hosts are superhosts, according to AirDNA.

To qualify as a superhost, you need to satisfy the following criteria over the past 365 days:
- host at least 10 stays per year
- a 90% response rate to inquiries within 24 hours
- a 50% review rate or higher
- a 4.8 average rating
- zero cancellations, except those under the extenuating circumstances policy.

Are you forced into instant book and short stays?

No, everything is voluntary. Allowing instant book is bad business for many VRs, such as larger remotely hosted properties where there is a risk of antisocial behavior by large groups. For these properties, a screening process is advisable before booking, even if it is just via messaging.

Similarly, short stays and one-night bookings are not practical where the cost of cleaning is high and it's logistically hard for cleaners to come daily. You need to set your minimum nights to suit your operation, even if you lose a few bookings in the process.

Similarly, you can set your cancellation policy any way you wish. It's a compromise between giving your guests easy cancellation options, versus your need to avoid last-minute guest cancellations. If you are getting lots of bookings, a strict cancellation policy would be appropriate.

Name

Include your VR name in the title to maximize your chances of guests finding you and booking direct on your website.

Pricing

It's a good tactic, as recommended by Airbnb, to offer lower prices when starting out, to get more bookings and a solid base of reviews. This should be temporary, and you should revert to normal prices when your reviews are solid. You will probably find that Airbnb suggests that average prices in your area are lower than yours. Check, but feel confident to ignore the suggestion.

If you have a premium VR, stick to your guns and price to the external market rate for a property of your quality. You are better off getting bookings by standing out from your competitors than just discounting your price!

Again, ignore Airbnb's suggested pricing model, especially if you have benchmarked your prices yourself.

Boost for new hosts

Though not explicitly acknowledged by Airbnb, there is strong anecdotal evidence to show that new hosts are given a ranking boost by the Airbnb algorithm to get some bookings early. If you are starting out, get everything ready including pricing and some good photos and exploit the early surge in booking inquiries if it occurs.

Keeping within the Airbnb system

Some Airbnb enthusiasts claim hosts should use Airbnb exclusively. This is nonsense, and smart VR owners wanting to maximize occupancy will list on multiple websites, putting more of their effort into operating the listings that give them the best returns.

Get to know the neighbors

It is more than courtesy to get to know your neighbors, it is in your interest. You can tell them you want responsible guests and you'll fix things if there is anything like loud noise. They can let you know if they have any concerns before they become legitimate complaints. In the first rental of my Richmond VR, the guests had an unauthorized gathering of 20 visitors, but fortunately I was on side with our neighbors who tipped me off. I spoke to the guests, who arranged for the visitors to leave quickly—much to my relief and the relief of the neighbors!

Working with neighbors has been particularly important for Airbnb VRs because of the astonishing pace of Airbnb growth. Early owners often operated outside the official local regulations without telling anyone. The neighbors would find a rental next door and feel blindsided with no one to talk to, resulting in exaggerated complaints to authorities, and blanket bans. It is far better to work proactively with neighbors and keep them on side, as the example above shows.

Stay tuned into Airbnb innovations

Airbnb is characterized by their constant innovation. In recent years they have added Trips, Business, China, Unique, B&Bs, Plus and Hotels. Some of these, like Business, are an opportunity. If you can satisfy the criteria for Business listings—like a CO_2 monitor, wi-fi and a desk—you will be ahead of your competitors.

> When I was at the 2015 Airbnb Paris Open, I wandered into their labs area and it was quickly apparent that they were simultaneously testing a dozen new products, several of which staff tested on me. They also spent an hour with me challenging suggestions I made until they got to their very essence. A fellow visitor was a vice-president of data for a major multinational and was trying to understand how Airbnb could be innovating on such a scale and pace. She was impressed.

In coming years, Airbnb will innovate in ways we can't predict now, so keep tuned into their changes, and exploit them!

Airbnb servicing

In recent years, there has been a surge in new businesses servicing Airbnb owners. Some provide a full service: taking bookings, organizing your account, organizing the key handover, and arranging the clean, all for a fee of 10%–30% of revenue. Airbnb even makes it easy for a service to manage multiple accounts with the owners' permission. For time-poor owners, this may be a useful option for a while.

The catch can be that such services thrive in an overheated market where demand exceeds supply, and a lot of overheated markets grow too fast, leading to short-term rental bans in places like New York and Barcelona. Always do your due diligence before starting.

> **Key takeaway: qualifying as an Airbnb superhost will mean you are doing well with most factors in the Airbnb ranking system.**

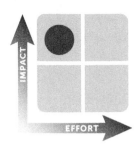

CHAPTER 36

Optimizing For HomeAway

KEY POINTS

- HomeAway ranking factors include reviews, declines, cancellations, response rate, instant book, calendar, price, appeal.
- HomeAway has a powerful set of tools to help you determine how you are faring compared to your competitors, and to discover ways of improving.
- Include your VR name in the title to maximize direct bookings to your own website.

How do you get listed higher in the HomeAway/ VRBO search results?

Like other online travel agencies, HomeAway doesn't publish its search algorithm, but does give some guidance. It also has an exceptional set of tools that VR owners can use to compare themselves to their competition, so they can self-diagnose how to improve.

Best match search

The algorithm assesses guest preferences from past behavior, e.g. prefers detached houses to condos. It then shows guests properties that match their preferences as well as specified dates, bedrooms, etc. These are ranked on various other factors listed below. This all means that ranking is complicated!

Ranking factors

Reviews, declines and cancellations, response rate, instant book, calendars, price, and appeal.

Many of these are reported back to you in your dashboard, so you can see how you are performing. There are few guidelines on most of these, whereas Airbnb gives implied guidance via eligibility criteria for superhost status.

Reviews

You should have at least 12 reviews, preferably recent, the higher the score the better. HomeAway has found properties having over 20 reviews will have 80% better performance than others. Clearly, asking guests directly will get you more reviews, and rating the guest will prompt them to review you. Clearly, giving them a great experience will score you higher.

Declines and cancellations

The fewer booking requests you decline, and the fewer times you cancel a booking, the better.

Response rate

You should respond to booking requests and inquiries within 24 hours. The faster you respond, the more professional you will appear to prospective guests.

Instant book on

Apparently, this will rank you higher. The system will also expose you to many Expedia searchers outside HomeAway.

As described for Airbnb, instant book may not be appropriate for larger properties and remote properties vulnerable to party guests, and owners should decide based on risk rather than a small chance of extra bookings.

Calendars

They should be updated frequently. If not updated for 60 days, ranking will suffer, and you may even be removed from the search results.

Price

Price is included in your ranking, particularly if you are way out of step with competitors. There is a pricing tool to help you see how the market is moving, e.g. for busy periods.

Appeal

How your listing appeals to guests won't be reflected in ranking but will impact the number of bookings you get. Factors include whether your title gets attention, whether your photos are high quality and make you stand out, whether your description is appealing, the facilities on offer, your host profile, your pricing, your minimum nights stay.

How do you know how you appeal to guests compared to your competition?

This is where HomeAway shines. It has several tools that show how you're performing compared to other listings in your area.

Win/loss cards

These posts in your feed show how you fared (won/lost) compared to another listing that was being considered by the same guest. If you lost, i.e. you weren't booked—great. You can look at the winner and see what they were offering compared to yourself. What was appealing? You can have a shot at figuring it out. All the way from title, description, and photos to pricing.

Comparative set

You can define a "comparative set" of properties similar to your own that you can compare yourself to on your dashboard. You can see how you are ranking on various factors compared to your set competitors. Any discrepancies, e.g. for your response rate, will help you work on things you can change.

Title

You can have a description 70 characters long. HomeAway suggests it be catchy, and it includes special facilities or local attractions. Yes, it's helpful to compare titles when you lose on your win/lose card.

Leakage via your property name

The big opportunity that is not mentioned by HomeAway, for obvious reasons, is to include your brand name in the title—e.g. "Milly's Place." That way, a smart prospective guest who doesn't want to pay a service fee can choose to not put in a booking request, but contact you direct via your own "Milly's Place" external website. That's "leakage" from the HomeAway system to you.

> **Key takeaway: HomeAway has a powerful set of tools to help you determine how you are faring compared to your competitors, and to discover ways of improving.**

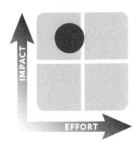

CHAPTER 37

Optimizing For Booking.com

> ## KEY POINTS
>
> - Review carefully the risks associated with the Booking. com instant book system before signing up, as there is no ability to refuse bookings.
> - There are tactics of relationship and cleaner presence to reduce risk for absent owners.
> - Reduce risk of last-minute cancellations with a strict cancellation policy.
> - Revenue can be increased by joining several partner programs for high performing listings.
> - There are ways to sidestep the oppressive price parity agreement.

Booking.com is a very different business to the other online travel agencies. It is almost entirely designed around a convenient guest experience, which has been a big factor in its market leadership for hotel guest bookings. The high volume of bookings, particularly for the European market, make it attractive to hotels and even VR owners. For many, the advantages of extra bookings outweigh the disadvantages.

However, the Booking.com system is not designed to make it easy for VR owners! The challenges for VRs are:

- *All* bookings are instant book.

- There is no dialogue with guests prior to booking and no way to decline a booking once you get to know the guest.
- The system encourages the ability for guests to cancel at the last minute without penalty.
- All listings are written by the Booking.com description writers. You have no say in what they write and no way to promote special experiences during the guest stay the way you can for other online travel agencies. However, they always list the name of your VR.
- The contract with the property owner usually requires price parity, forcing the owner to not advertise anywhere a price lower than that on the Booking.com listing.
- The owner takes all payments, and credit cards are often declined in the weeks and months after the original booking is made.

As with the other OTAs, the ranking algorithm is not revealed, but it seems that the general principles for the algorithm are:

- More frequently booked properties are ranked higher than local competitors.
- Better reviews help you rank higher.
- Properties available at a 10%–15% discount to "Genius" club guests have a higher exposure and get more bookings.
- Higher commissions paid get you ranked higher.

The deck seems firmly stacked against the VR owner, but there are some things VR owners can do to optimize their use of Booking.com.

Firstly, if you are exposed to high risk through the system, don't use the Booking.com platform! For example, large remote properties where there is no representative onsite are vulnerable to damage from party guests.

If you do decide to list with Booking.com, make sure you stand out from your competitors.

Stand out

- Make sure all your facilities are shown on your listing and are accurate.
- Have excellent photographs that make your property stand out.

Reviews

Like all online travel agencies, you should encourage your guests to submit reviews through the system, particularly the ones who have a great experience. The more reviews the better; the higher rating the better.

Challenge the description

If there are aspects in your description that have been missed, go back to Support and tell them, and offer a suggested change. I have done that successfully where our ocean view was omitted from the original description. I pointed out the omission, using a number of quotes from past Booking.com guest reviews who loved the ocean view, so it was the customer saying it, not just me. I made it easy to make the change with new suggested wording, and it was changed the next day.

Select a strict cancellation policy

The guest culture is to expect to be able to cancel at the last minute. The system default is last-minute cancellation, but you can set a stricter cancellation policy to avoid late cancellations, e.g. where the guest loses their payment if they cancel within six weeks of the stay.

Join the preferred partner and genius programs

The **preferred partner program** is offered to the top 30% of listings meeting criteria of good availability, low cancellations, on-time invoice payments, a review score of 7.0 or more. Those in the program are given higher rankings and extra visibility via a thumbs-up sign. Booking.com claims this results in up to 35% more bookings. You can see if you are eligible via the Opportunities tab. My contacts report that this gives excellent results.

You can join the **genius program** by discounting your cheapest room by 10%, if you have five or more reviews, a review score over 7.5, and you are among the top 50% performers in your area. Those in the program are exposed to genius-program guests who book more and pay more. Booking.com claims this results in 17% more revenue, after taking into account the discounted price. Again, you can see if you are eligible via the Opportunities tab.

Reduce risk

If no one is onsite, encourage your cleaner to cruise past occasionally and report any potential issues, like more cars and people onsite than for the booking.

After the booking is received, have a chat with the guest to make a relationship. Use the power of the crowd referred to in the Psychology chapter to set expectations. "We are a small business and so lucky that guests like you invariably look after the property. Thank you for choosing us."

If you have a guest you are uncertain about and their card is declined at time of payment, you can report the non-payment and request that the booking be cancelled. In most cases it will be.

Sidestep the price parity clause

In some countries, such as Australia and some European nations, the price parity clause has been found to be anti-competitive. In those countries, lower pricing on the owner's website is allowed for loyalty discounts. In Australia, the owner can set any price for phone inquiries to the owner's own website.

Given the growing market dominance of Booking.com, consumer authorities are likely to further water down the price parity clause, as anti-competitive behavior is clearer.

Hotels with hundreds of rooms are easily scrutinized for keeping to the parity rule. However, many hundreds of sole-owner VRs who are confused about price parity anyway are harder to scrutinize. A smaller owner is likely to set any price they want and if challenged, reasonably say they are confused by the complex 11,400-word agreement. Any crackdown on an individual owner would attract publicity and public outrage at the oppression of a small owner by a giant player and would possibly trigger a review of anti-competitive behavior by authorities.

Take care with no-shows

If there is a no-show, you need to formally log it in the Booking.com system within the time frame (48 hours), or you will be charged a commission on someone who cancelled at the last minute, a tough double whammy.

> Key takeaway: review carefully the risks associated with the Booking.com instant book system before signing up, as there is no ability to refuse bookings.

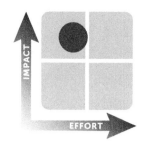

CHAPTER 38

Optimizing For TripAdvisor

> **KEY POINTS**
> - TripAdvisor listings for vacation rentals are made via FlipKey, a subsidiary.
> - Anecdotal advice is that FlipKey delivers fewer bookings than the other big four online travel agencies.
> - Similar optimization principles apply to Airbnb and HomeAway.

TripAdvisor is the unchallenged market leader for reviews as a source of information for travelers when researching a vacation.

Fuzzy business model

However, when it comes to bookings it's a different story, due to its confused business model:

- A separate subsidiary brand, FlipKey, operates vacation rentals in a close copy of the Airbnb model—free to list, small 3% owner booking fee, large 10%+ guest service fee, reciprocal reviews.
- A listing-only fee applies to some categories, and it allows a direct link to a website. The categories include hotels and B&Bs and specialty lodgings, and are fuzzy.

The reality is vacation rentals will have to list on FlipKey—or HolidayLettings in the UK. The anecdotal advice from other VR owners is that FlipKey delivers fewer bookings than the other three big online travel agencies. It may be that FlipKey does well in some areas, so as advised in Chapter 8, check with your colleagues and network to see how FlipKey is performing in your area.

Given the lack of performance data, I haven't listed on FlipKey, but I keep an open mind, and I may list if there is solid evidence of local performance.

Optimizing FlipKey

The principles to optimize for TripAdvisor are much the same as for similar online travel agency models, i.e. Airbnb and HomeAway:

- Get early bookings by lowering price.
- Build bookings and reviews.
- Consider instant book.
- Initially adopt flexible house rules and tighten up later.

> Key takeaway: similar optimization principles apply to Airbnb and HomeAway.

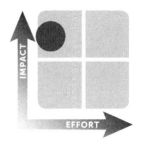

Optimizing Your Prices

> **KEY POINTS**
>
> - It's easy to leave pricing unchanged through complacency and lose bookings or lose margin.
> - One hour spent benchmarking the market on price is likely to be the most valuable hour you will spend all year.
> - Resist the online travel agency messages telling you your pricing needs to change to meet the average local market.
> - While OTA pricing models can give good hints about seasonal changes, you need to be well organized to document all your pricing decisions.

There are several pathways with pricing, which can lead you to different outcomes. The following is the good pathway. Initially, after starting operation, you will set prices low to attract a quick following of happy guests. After you've steadily become popular and well booked, you will have a hard look at competitor pricing and adjust your prices up. In the next few years you meet that happy sweet spot where prices are low enough for high occupancy and a good return, but not so high that the price scares away potential guests.

The complacency trap

The less desirable pathway is complacency and neglect. It is easy to leave your prices static or adjusted for inflation for several years, while the market is shifting around you. In some locations, vacation rentals are becoming more sought-after; you may be already fully booked, and you can leave a lot of money on the table by keeping your prices too low. If you are reading this book, chances are you already have an outstanding property and are finding more ways to add value and stand out from the market.

Once I was fully booked, I tried putting up prices by 10%—no change in demand—then nine months later another 10%—no change in demand—and the next year another 10%. The last saw a slight softening in demand, and the sweet spot. I should probably have moved earlier! Each time I checked prices it took just an hour to check out competitors in the market, their prices, and their occupancy.

Each time I increased annual net return by around A\$8,000. Not bad for an hour of work.

As explained in the Basics section, it's easy to get confused, so you need to be organized with your own reference file that documents public holidays, seasonal changes, and your pricing decisions for each site you list on.

> One hour spent benchmarking prices against your competitors may be the highest-value hour you ever spend on your VR

The online travel agency push to drop prices

The perfect OTA world is to have a growing market of VR suppliers, all undercutting themselves, all at a low price that will increase demand. That is, a low-priced commodity giving them increasing profits.

You will inevitably get "suggestions" from OTAs saying the average for your area is well below your price and you should consider lowering your prices. Think about this. If you are reading this book, chances are that you have an outstanding property performing well above the market average, and the OTA "suggestions" based on averages are irrelevant. You should make your own decisions based on your unique situation.

On the other hand, several OTAs have pricing tools to help you stay competitive for seasonal pricing changes and are worth checking periodically.

Stay agile

While it's great to find your sweet spot with pricing, you need to stay agile and keep an eye on the market. This is particularly important with the advent of Airbnb, which makes it easy for all those moms and pops out there to list as a VR rental. A few photos and an hour on the Airbnb site, and they are up and running.

Globally, Airbnb has grown listing supply by 100% year on year for many years. In some areas the competition has doubled and tripled, and the prices are pushing lower and lower.

In these areas you need to keep your eye on the ball. You may need to lower your price to stay highly occupied. You certainly need to find ways to stand out and provide good value for your price.

> Spend an hour benchmarking prices every six months

> Key takeaway: one hour spent benchmarking the market on price is likely to be the most valuable hour you will spend all year.

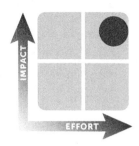

Search Engine Optimization

KEY POINTS

- VR owners can use search engine optimization to bring more guests to their website and book direct.

- While it is impractical for VRs to rank for the most common search phrases, it is feasible to rank for less usual, or "long tail," keywords.

- SEO is quite specialized, requiring extra skills, application and long-term persistence.

Search engine optimization, or SEO, is a fancy phrase meaning simply **helping the search engines find your website better than other sites.** In our internet-dominated world, the websites that are ranked highest by the search engines win more business, and that is particularly true for our vacation rental world. It is logical then that SEO is a highly competitive activity between competing businesses. It is hard to do well, due to the intense competition out there. The big players, like online travel agencies with big resources, will—generally—perform better in SEO than small players like individual vacation rental owners, but not always.

In practical terms "search engine" means Google, due to its market dominance. Google has one overarching principle in how it ranks websites. It wants to give users "the best user experience possible."

> Here be dragons ...

In the fierce world of SEO, there are many SEO "experts" looking for shortcuts to fool Google and get ahead of their competition. Google, on the other hand, is constantly changing its algorithm to root out shortcuts and reward a genuinely good user experience. It has been said that the Google ranking algorithm has become so complex that no one person in Google fully understands it!

What does this mean for the small VR owner?

You need to be realistic and accept that the big online travel agencies with their extra teams working full-time on SEO will get their websites ranking higher for the more common search terms than the small VR owner can for their small website. However, the small owner with specialist knowledge in a small local niche can do well.

For example, the keyword searches "accommodation location" and "vacation rental location" will be fully covered by the big websites, and you don't stand a chance of getting found.

However, "long tail," or unusual, search phrases with two to five keywords are less likely to be well covered by the online travel agencies, and the small owner may compete successfully. This is particularly for topics of local interest that searchers may be looking for *before* they even think of booking some accommodation. As a local, you are very well placed to know the special local attractions and all the local answers for researchers.

The overall tactic is to write some pages of content on your website that will be found by prospective guests researching the area. They find your content, and they discover that you offer accommodation, then they ask you for a direct booking.

For example, consider a holiday rental in Lorne, a summer seaside resort south of Melbourne. The obvious simple accommodation keyword phrases like "accommodation lorne" and "getaways in lorne" are likely to be dominated by many other websites, and it's futile trying to rank for them.

However, some long-tail phrase searches used by prospective guests during the research stage might be:

- surfing near lorne
- best beaches in lorne
- restaurants in lorne
- places to eat in lorne
- drives from lorne
- where can I fish near lorne?
- dog friendly beaches near lorne.

Now armed with the realistic target keyword phrases, the small owner can start optimizing their website for them.

How do you optimize for target keyword phrases?

You need to provide lots of good content on your website for your target phrases. That usually means pages or blog posts on your website specifically targeted to those keyword phrases.

It doesn't mean combine everything on one page. The content should be separate, on separate pages. That way Google can see you have specific helpful content for that topic and Google can show your website high in the search results for those keywords.

For example, you can write a post on your website relevant to each long-tail phrase. For the phrase "best beaches in lorne" you might make post to your website titled "A guide to the best beaches in Lorne." For the phrase "restaurants in lorne" you might make a post to your website titled "Guide to restaurants and eating out in Lorne." You might link to most of them.

It also helps if other websites give your site authority by providing links back to your website. For example, a local pub or shop might link to your website if you explain that you have featured them on your website. It all helps Google to build a picture that you are a helpful, trusted resource for your target keyword phrases.

Good content is also why I like a newsletter; you can create keyword rich content in each edition of your newsletter and post each newsletter as a blog post. It can also be fun.

It also probably helps if your website is listed on Google My Business, and you are getting reviews posted to your My Business listing. See Chapter 30. And it probably helps if there are social media signals around your website and your target phrases. This is more fuzzy. It also takes Google a while to trust you and your content. It may take days, weeks, or not happen at all!

Will SEO work for you?

The harsh reality is that you may be doing all the right things, the right target keywords, the right content in the right places—but there are no guarantees that you will succeed in ranking high in Google or in getting direct bookings from it!

That is why SEO is a high-effort, moderate-impact activity. It is good to do it later in your journey, after you have all the basics in place; that way, if it works it is a bonus, not something you are relying on.

> **Key takeaway:** VR owners can use search engine optimization to bring more guests to their website and book direct.

CHAPTER 41

Insiders' Expert Guides

KEY POINTS

- As a local VR owner, you have authority as an expert that is valued by your guests.
- You can provide added value to your guests by giving them an *insider's guide* to local attractions and food.
- The guide helps guest loyalty and your SEO authority.

One very good way to provide extra value for your guests is to be the local expert who gives them tips to make their stay happier and more satisfying. Chances are you have been living in or visiting the area for many years, and you genuinely have discovered the best local experiences. The best museums. The restaurant with the best food. The café with the best coffee. The best place to go fishing. The best local attractions to see. The hidden foodie gem found after an interesting drive through the area. In a city, how best to use the transport system.

From long experience, about half the guests who hear your local recommendations will try them and thank you afterwards.

To make this easier for your guests, you can develop your own "insider's guide." It may be just one guide, or it may be multiple. I have three. A food lovers' guide. A local attractions guide. Tips for dog owners. Guests often say, "Thank you for the guides. I read them all, and I'm so excited I can't wait."

You should start simple, like with a general local guide, and add more as you test your guests' needs, as described in the earlier Customer Obsession chapter. You can send a pdf to your guests on booking, and you can have a copy inside your rental. You can also give away the guide to prospective guests on the reciprocation principle—you help, they feel more obligation to book. (Refer to the earlier chapter on psychology.)

I first heard the term "**insider's guide**" from my friend and VR guru Matt Landau. Though I had been producing my own local guide, the "**insider's guide**" name has a special magic of exclusivity about it. Matt can be found at Vrmb.com.

SEO benefits

You can even publish your guide on your website for luring new guests. Once published it will provide valuable SEO strength to your website. As you become more experienced, you can add niche guides to your website to provide the highly valuable niche SEO that can compete more effectively than an OTA.

Won't competitors copy my guide?

Lazy competitors might try copying your material, but there is an easy deterrent: sprinkle your VR name brand throughout your guide. "The Red Door guide to Localsville," "just 10 minutes walk from Red Door," "at Red Door we have been visiting this restaurant for years," "they give a discount if you say you are from Red Door." Of course, your brand name should also be in the footer. The document should be pdf to make selective text copying harder.

How to build your guide

1. Think through your top local experiences (say, the top 10) and write about them naturally as if you were speaking to a friend, putting the text in a Word file.

2. Choose an image for each experience where it helps provide interest.

3. Images should be a modest size and edited to 50–100kb in file size *before* being added to the Word file—so you don't end up with a clumsily huge document. Do not skip this step!

4. Ensure your VR brand name is sprinkled naturally through the document, and in your title page and footer, so it can't be copied in entirety.

5. Test the final draft on some friends or guests.

6. Save the final version as a pdf, and check that the file size is modest. (If over one megabyte, compress using the handy free site www.smallpdf.com and if necessary reduce the image sizes.)

You can print the final copy, put it inside your property and keep a copy handy to email to inquiring guests. You can put a copy on your website so you are seen by the world as the local expert!

Over time you can add more guides on local topics, and Google will love it, as will searching guests.

Electronic guides—or not?

There is a growing number of places you can put guides like tablets, apps, and other software. I am not a fan. The key rule is to "keep it simple" and low-tech so any guest can read it in seconds with no extra skills. Guests are there to enjoy their holiday, not to battle with new technology. The exception is where your target customers are tech-hungry millennials, in which case you would use an electronic guide on an in-house tablet.

Of course, once you email your **insider's guide** to your guests, they can access it electronically on their phone any time when they are out and about.

Insider's guide as a lead magnet for newsletter sign-up

For the more adventurous marketer, you can use the guide as a lead magnet, or lure, to get prospective guests to sign up for your newsletter. They get the guide, and you get them on your list of prospective guests to whom you send information and marketing material. You can even use Google ads to promote the guide.

However, this is all fairly advanced, and initially I suggest you keep it simple—just give away the guide to your guests and put it on your website for SEO value.

> **Key takeaway: you can provide added value to your guests by giving them an insider's guide to local attractions and food.**

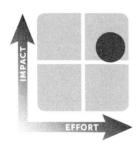

CHAPTER 42

Google Ads

> ## KEY POINTS
> - Google Ads is another way to drive traffic to your website.
> - While the online travel agencies have bid up the most common Google advertising phrases, a small VR owner can be competitive on the less well known phrases.
> - Take it slowly, and don't be afraid to ask for professional help.
> - Keep ads until later in your journey.

The Google Ads advertising system, formerly known as AdWords[1] is how Google makes its money. It is projected that Google will have revenue of about $130 billion in 2018, and the travel and tourism industry is one of its biggest revenue sources (MarketScreener 2018). In practical terms, that includes a huge contribution from the online travel agencies.

How it works

When someone searches for accommodation in your area, they may use a phrase like "vacation rentals smallsville," and a list of websites

---

1 Google AdWords was renamed Google Ads in June 2018 as part of a reorganization of their advertising system.

come up to help the searcher. At the top of the list of search results are about four advertisements labeled "Ads."

When the searcher clicks on one of those Google ads, the advertiser pays Google a small fee, typically $2. The more popular search phrases cost a lot more; the less popular phrases cost less. The more the advertiser sets for their clicks, the higher the ad is listed on the search results. In the low season, the "cost per click" drops, by maybe $1, and in the high season it increases to maybe $20, and every location is different.

In many places, the online travel agencies have simply bid higher for clicks than anyone else, making it uneconomic for small VR operators to use Google Ads effectively.

However, all is not lost. As you probably know your customers better than the OTAs, you may discover that many of your guests will be searching for a niche, such as fishing, bike riding, bird-watching, etc. Let's say it is fishing. A small operator could run some Google Ads for "fishing smallsville" and pay a fraction of the cost per click compared to accommodation-related ads.

Around 10 years ago I found a few niches like the pet market that were inexpensive, and my Google Ads advertising was very successful in bringing in a lot of business to my VRs. I ran Google Ads for many years and helped colleagues set up Google Ads in several industries, but since the domination of the online travel agencies—no longer!

Size of your VR business is important

Google Ads is very effective if you are responsible for many VRs in the same area. For example, an online travel agency may have 100 properties in one area, and the cost of clicking on one ad is spread over those 100 properties.

For a small VR operator with one or two properties in the same area, such as the target readership of this book, the cost can only be spread over that couple of properties, and the cost per ad can be quite high and not cost-effective. For this example, the OTA would have a 100 to 2 cost advantage!

For property managers running 20 or so properties in an area, Google Ads may well be quite effective.

Not for the inexperienced user

Google has done a good job of making it easy to sign up and start running ads. However, as the system has grown more sophisticated, so has its complexity. There are tips and guidelines, but it takes a lot of concentration and experimentation to master the system.

It is like a racing car. It is complicated. It can be expensive to run and driven by an expert it can go faster than the competition, but for an inexperienced driver it can be dangerous and run off the track, injuring the driver.

For example, an inexperienced Google Ads user could inadvertently set up an ad for a general search term like "vacation rental," run the ad worldwide on a daily budget of $1,000, and spend $10,000 in 10 days!

> Google Ads is like a racing car: in the hands of an expert it can accelerate past the competition, but handled by the inexperienced it can be dangerous!

Professional help is available

If you are serious about trying Google Ads, the easy way is to get some help from a professional company with a strict budget. Companies advertise as "search marketing" or "pay-per-click advertising" provide these services. You might like to try it for your VR, but you should wait until you have your basics right and even have some of the more advanced operations running, like a loyalty scheme, email marketing, **insider guides** and website.

DIY?—Yes, you can!

Despite all the warnings, many VR owners are very talented, having acquired advanced skills in a prior profession, and some folks just love a challenge! If that is you, by all means have a go at Google Ads. Buy a book, take it slow, and gradually you too can become an expert in Google Ads, like anything else.

I have run my own Google Ads campaigns for years, and in the early years I even helped others run theirs. For the technically minded like me, it was great fun. Now I write books!

That is the wonderful thing about operating a VR: you run a small business and you are your own boss. You can try anything!

> Key takeaway: while the online travel agencies have bid up the most common Google advertising phrases, a small VR owner can be competitive on the less well known phrases.

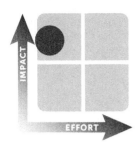

CHAPTER 43

Managed Services

KEY POINTS

- VR management companies offer excellent services to manage your entire operation, but the net return is modest.
- Some new companies will manage your property solely on Airbnb.
- Many owners and readers of this book will prefer to manage everything themselves, with just the support of a good local cleaner.

When you are remote from your VR, you need to get local help. There is a choice of models for running your VR, from using a fully managed service to just using a cleaner and doing the rest yourself.

A good solution can be to engage a management company, particularly in the early days while you are figuring out how it all works. I did just that in the early days of our Treetops VR, when we were remote our corporate jobs kept us short of time. The local management company did an excellent job in managing the bookings and arranging the cleaning and emergency maintenance; I did extra marketing for extra bookings and creative changes to the property so it was more attractive. The company charged a fair commission for their services and glued it all together so it ran very well. Most management companies will want total control of marketing, guests and cleaning, and that's a good model too.

Commissions charged vary widely in the industry from 20%–30% plus cleaning and consumables, plus online travel agency fees, so you will usually net under half the fees your guests pay to stay in your VR.

A new model has emerged with the growth of Airbnb—companies that service just Airbnb properties. They manage the Airbnb account, the bookings, the cleaning, the greeting, and key handover. The standardization of the Airbnb processes makes managing easy. For many owners this is a good solution too. For some, owning a VR is a real estate play all about capital gain, so net revenue is secondary, and a managed model is ideal.

Most readers of this book will want to manage most of the operation themselves and maximize net returns. For this model, you will rely heavily on your cleaner and maintenance person, so the importance of a suitable cleaner can't be overestimated. You can run an excellent VR, have total control, and take every opportunity to maximize your bookings.

You can also contract out admin services to a virtual assistant, or VA, sometimes local, sometimes in a remote, low-cost country like the Philippines. VAs are very helpful for things such as social media, websites, and SEO. I used a VA from Philippines for my websites, with mixed results.

So, many models, many choices—it's up to you to decide what works best for you!

> **Key takeaway:** VR management companies offer excellent services to manage your entire operation, but the net return is modest.

PART 3

**ADVANCED TECHNIQUES
FOR MASTERY**

SECTION 4

HIGH VALUE-ADD EXTRAS

CHAPTER 44

Knowledge Sources

KEY POINTS

- Knowledge is the key to success in the VR industry.
- A list of valuable resources is given for owners to use, with my recommendations for the most useful.

The key to vacation rental mastery is knowledge. When I started Sea Zen and attained 90% occupancy within three months in the hard winter season, the key was the knowledge I had accumulated over 12 years.

When a VR guru was asked what he would do differently if starting again, he wisely said he'd get more knowledge by going to some conferences and networking with experts—and spend more time on the important things. How do you know what the important things are? Knowledge!

Books like this are one source of knowledge, and I hope it is valuable for you. I also have a newsletter, courses, and e-books at www.holidayrentalmastery.com.

Other sources of knowledge include training courses, thought leaders, conferences, newsletters, e-books, forums, podcasts. Mastermind groups, covered in the next chapter, are another fabulous knowledge source.

Thought leaders—people to learn from

Matt Landau, based in Panama, is outstanding. He has a closed forum called the Inner Circle, a community of VR innovators, with courses, pdfs, e-books. He also has a newsletter/blog, a podcast series, and a video series: www.vrmb.com.

I met Matt in Panama in 2013 and stayed at his VR. He took us on a tour of his social program, which finds work for local street gang members. We talked about the future of the industry, and it was clear then he had a strong vision for the future. He was nurturing his online VR owner community called the Inner Circle, which has grown since to be a leading incubator of VR innovation.

He continues to break new ground with concepts such as Limited Edition—original innovations by VR owners to provide unique experiences for their guests that can't be replicated by the big online travel agencies. His *Sense of Place* video series showcases VR innovators all around the world.

Heather Bayer, based in Ontario, Canada. She has a superb podcast called *Vacation Rental Success* with over 250 episodes. Her podcast keeps a good balance between high-level strategy and down-to-earth guest experiences that she tussles with as owner of an Ontario VR management company running over 200 widely dispersed properties. Everything from remote sensing gadgets to AVROA, the Association of Vacation Rental Operators and Affiliates, where she heads the learning arm.

She also runs the outstanding Vacation Rental Success Summit, an annual conference for VR independent operators. She also has books, courses, the Vacation Rental Formula membership group, and a newsletter. See www.cottageblogger.com.

There are many others, like Alan Egan, David Angotti, Steve Milo, Tyann Marcink, Jasper Ribbers, Antonio Bortolotti, and more, but Matt and Heather stand out.

Conferences for VR operators

- Vacation Rental Success Summit organized by Heather Bayer and Mike Bayer, usually in North America: www.vacationrentalsuccesssummit.com.
- Vacation Rental World Summit organized by Antonio Bortolotti, usually in Europe: www.vacationrentalworldsummit.com/.
- Vacation Rental Managers Association. For VR managers, but small VR operators can sometimes attend. Huge conferences at various venues and times during the year: www.vrma.org.

Your local tourism organization may have useful conferences, and although not fine-tuned to VR operators, will be a networking opportunity.

Podcasts

- *Vacation Rental Success*, by Heather Bayer: www.cottageblogger.com
- *Unlocked*, by Matt Landau: www.vrmb.com/unlocked-podcast
- *Get Paid for Your Pad*, by Jasper Ribbers. Airbnb theme: www.getpaidforyourpad.com
- *Holiday Let Success*, by Elaine Watts. UK-based: www.holidayletsuccess.com

Newsletters

Almost all the folks mentioned above have newsletters. There are some run by the large vendors and organizations offering services to VR operators.

Skift is an outstanding daily newsletter with international news on a broad range of topics from travel to accommodation: www.skift.com. *Smarthosts* curates a weekly digest of interesting VR articles. UK-based: www.smarthosts.org.

You should be guarded in viewing newsletters from online travel agencies. They are pushing a viewpoint.

In the rapidly changing world of vacation rentals, you may want to get several sources of information. Try several newsletters and a podcast, and prune back to a few that work for you. You might like to sign up to my newsletter at Holidayrentalmastery.com.

Creative cross-pollination

It is a good policy to have a few knowledge sources outside your core interests as a stimulus for creative thinking. Often reading about or listening to someone trying new ideas can trigger a related idea that you can use to experiment with in your VR business. The same applies to exploring a different industry—new ideas come at the most unexpected times.

When you are looking to find ways to stand out from your competition, new ideas and experiments are gold.

> Key takeaway: there are many valuable information sources to help owners improve.

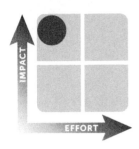

CHAPTER 45

Mastermind

KEY POINTS

- A mastermind group of highly motivated owners in the VR industry is one of the most valuable activities a VR owner can take part in.
- The mastermind group can accelerate learning and keep you on top of shifting trends.
- You can form your own mastermind group.

A mastermind group is a small number of people meeting regularly to share ideas on improvement. *It is one of the most powerful activities that I take part in and costs nothing but time.* I'm in several. In the VR industry, the mastermind idea is to get several highly motivated owners together to share problems and solutions and find ways of improving their businesses.

Forming a mastermind

I formed my first group in 2013 after I met some owners at a conference who had just won an award. Over drinks, it became clear that they were innovators who I could learn from, and they could also learn from me. They also lived within an hour's drive. We all clicked. Back home, I sought out the person in my local market who was innovating most and proposed to him and the other two that we form a mastermind group.

They all jumped at the chance, and we started meeting once a month. Later, as we chomped through topics, we met less frequently, about once in three months.

We also know each other well enough to pick up the phone in a crisis and get another mature viewpoint—very valuable in an industry where owners often work alone.

How a mastermind works

A chairperson puts together a loose agenda with a target topic or problem before the meeting. At the meeting, each contributes their ideas on the problem, and invariably something will come out of left field that several in the group benefit from.

Also, each person takes turn to give a brief update on how they are going. Some wins, a problem they are working on, and the universal topic—Which online travel agencies have been giving the best results since the last meeting?

The group might agree on a common problem or individual problem to discuss at the next meeting.

A mastermind meeting takes one to two hours face to face, usually over coffee in a quiet café, and is informal. It can also be held virtually on Skype. My group has also toured each other's VR properties, asked lots of questions, and made suggestions.

Guidelines for a mastermind

1. Form your group from highly motivated VR business owners local to the area.
2. Start small.

3. Select a permanent or rotating chair to organize each meeting at an agreed frequency.
4. Have a main topic or one party's specific problem on the agenda for each meeting.
5. At each meeting, share current business conditions/short-term trends/personal wins or issues.
6. Information revealed is private to the meeting and not to be revealed externally without the other parties' permission. That way, everyone can talk freely about even the most embarrassing problem.
7. If a new person is introduced, they should not become permanent until the prior group is comfortable with the dynamics. Dysfunctional personalities will kill the group.

Competitors or colleagues?

The VR industry is big enough that a direct competitor can become a colleague in a mastermind without materially affecting other members' bookings. The threat to business is not a from a single local competitor; it is from complacency, inaction, and getting left behind as the industry morphs around you.

Examples of mastermind topics

- cleaning, linen, consumables, comparisons of local suppliers
- which marketing methods are working best, where recent bookings are coming from—direct bookings versus the individual online travel agencies
- shifts in OTA operations and rule changes
- state of the current market. Number of forward bookings. Is a lull a temporary blip for one operator or a general downturn in the market? Is the market strong enough to raise prices? Is there a trend for more couples, or families, or overseas visitors? Short stays or long stays?

- conversion tactics and sharing each other's scripts. Reviews tactics
- Google Ads, Facebook, newsletters, loyalty tactics, social media experiments
- difficult guests, complaints tactics.

My groups have discussed all these and more. It can be comforting to have a friendly shoulder to lean on and someone to commiserate with when things get tough!

Power of group data

By sharing current business trends across the group, the amount of data triples and quadruples. A short-term blip for one operator can quickly be seen as a regional trend (or not), so the appropriate changes can be made well ahead of competitors. An apparent trend toward short bookings may be revealed as an anomaly that can be safely ignored.

Most highly motivated operators will be running an experiment or two, sometimes over many months. If each of the group shares their experiments, they can innovate at an astonishing rate.

It is an effort to list with a new online travel agency that may take many months to produce a stable stream of bookings. Should one person make the change? If the others in the group have already tried that OTA and are getting results (or not), the decision is easy.

Non-VR mastermind

Not only can you benefit from VR colleagues in your industry, you can also form a business mastermind with others facing business issues in entirely different industries. This is particularly helpful for tax, accounting, financials, internet marketing, offline marketing virtual assistants, etc.

> I have short regular phone sessions with a colleague in an entirely different industry, where our problems and experiments help each other surprisingly often. We coach each other to stay accountable for our goals. It is a very powerful motivator.

Barriers to entry

Starting a mastermind is a little challenging. You put a proposal to someone you may not know very well to do something quite unusual. Will you be rejected? Probably not, but the fear of doing something new is hard for all of us, a real barrier to entry into a new state.

In reality, it will not be difficult, and remember any barrier to entry is wonderful—once you are through the barrier you will be well ahead of your competitors!

> **Key takeaway: a mastermind group of highly motivated owners in the VR industry is one of the most valuable activities a VR owner can take part in.**

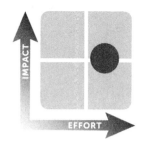

CHAPTER 46

Publicity

KEY POINTS
- Journalist publicity can help drive more bookings but takes dedicated time and effort.
- The approach is to follow target journalists, help them, and eventually offer an interesting story with an angle for publication.

There are enough tools in this book to help you become highly booked without publicity, and it's not something I would recommend for owners of just a few rentals. However, some creative VR owners with 5–10 listings have found that publicity can help their business.

Target journalists over time

The approach taken by several VR owners is to keep a record of all the journalists and bloggers in their market and build a spreadsheet of target writers over a period of 3–12 months.

They then choose a few writers and start to engage with feedback on their pieces and offer information from the owner's own markets. Eventually, the hope is for a value exchange where the owners provide value to the writers and the writers feature the property in an article. It takes time and persistence, with no guarantee of a payoff.

To get attention, writers need a fresh story with a fresh angle that is different. You should have the bones of a story ready that would make for interesting copy.

Competitions

Sometimes there are competitions run by regional associations or even by online travel agencies. Some have a most popular category, and enterprising owners I know go all out to contact past guests to get their endorsement and have sometimes won the competition and reaped the publicity reward.

If you do get coverage, you can then use that as a credential of authority on your website. "As reported in the Bugle," "winner of the most popular romantic rental," etc. You can also approach your local newspaper and tell them you have won an award and get coverage there.

Contacts

It is amazing how deep your existing contacts can reach. We are only a few degrees of separation from most people on the planet. Ask your contacts if they know any travel journalists or who would know some travel journalists. Once you make contact simply ask for advice on how you might get publicity—not a direct request for them to publicize you—and you may get some good advice on the next steps and maybe a story.

The publicity path is not easy; good luck if you want to give it a try.

> **Key takeaway: journalist publicity can help drive more bookings but takes dedicated time and effort.**

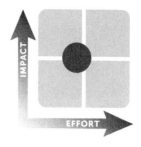

CHAPTER 47

Offline Marketing

> **KEY POINTS**
> - Offline advertising is often overlooked but handy for getting extra bookings.
> - Ads at shops for your target niche can be useful—like at the vet for dog lovers.
> - Letterbox drops can help get bookings from locals who want somewhere for visiting family.
> - Always ask guests how they found you after they book!

The VR world doesn't just live on the internet! If you understand your guest niches well, you will find that they often go to the same physical space and they spend time reading ordinary paper notices. If you know those places, you can advertise your offer to them very effectively. Here are some examples of offline marketing to give you some ideas.

Business cards

You can inexpensively have 500 business cards made with a picture featuring your VR, your website, and your contact details. As you meet folks socially, they will often genuinely be interested in your VR and want to know more. You just hand over your card; they research your website and book with you.

Dog-lover niche

You can put a flyer or a postcard on the noticeboard at your local vet in the nearest city, feeding your VR with guests. Or at your local dog groomer. The message is, "Dogs like going on holidays too." You have a great picture, a short message, and your phone and website. The business owners may even allow you to leave some business cards there too.

I had the president of the Scottish Terrier Club come to stay, and she loved the experience. She wrote a story in the club newsletter, and I had several other members come and stay. I also put some catchy postcards in our local vet with some bonus bookings.

Other niche businesses

If you have surfers come to your VR from the city, put up an ad in your feeder city surf shop. If your market is for families with children, you can put an ad on the school noticeboard with whom you have a connection in the major feeder city.

The work noticeboard

Your colleagues will hear your stories of your VR and want to find out more. There is often a noticeboard at work for selling furniture and advertising social events, which you can use. In large workplaces, a lot of people will see your notice and may even prefer to book with someone from work who they know and trust. Your raving fans can be sometimes such enthusiastic advocates they will volunteer to put up your flyer at work!

In the early days of Treetops, the owner had half his bookings through staff of a major television station, starting with one guest who just loved the property and sold it to their colleagues.

Letterbox drop for visiting local families

A lot of VRs are in urban locations, and many families come from interstate to visit. They want to be close, but not too close, so the local family and their visitors each have their own private space. This happened a lot when we operated our Richmond townhouse VR in inner Melbourne. It was particularly useful for families when Mom came to visit her daughter for the daughter's firstborn.

How do you advertise locally? Simple: the letterbox drop. Print postcards with an image and details of your VR and have them delivered to all the neighbors' letterboxes a few times a year. My fabulous local cleaner, Lizzie, thought it was a hoot and volunteered to deliver the postcards on her way home.

> I once asked a well-booked VR colleague in a prosperous urban area which online travel agencies she used. She said, "Just one, but most of my business comes from local letterbox drops, and my neighbors don't care what they pay for their families to visit locally!"

Ads on cars

Many VR owners operate remotely from their rental. When you live in the same catchment as your target guests, it makes sense to put an ad on your car as you drive around surrounded by prospective guests. It would be worth trying: a magnetic advertising sign attached to your car is inexpensive compared to the online travel agency commissions you are paying, and may be a good investment.

Experiment and measure

Don't forget to *always* ask that question for new bookings: "And how did you find us?" Otherwise how will you know which of your offline marketing is working?

> **Key takeaway: offline advertising is often overlooked but handy for getting extra bookings.**

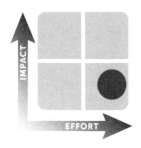

CHAPTER 48

Social Media

> **KEY POINTS**
> - There have been mixed messages over the effectiveness of social media in obtaining VR bookings.
> - It may be best to wait and observe before jumping in deep with social media, unless you are using it personally anyway.
> - If SEO is important for you, social media will probably be helpful.

You might be wondering why this chapter has been left so far back in this book. It is because I haven't seen much hard evidence of social media working for actually getting bookings for VR rentals, nor much hard evidence at conferences for high-volume sign-ups from social media. Many folks out there offer their social media services, but I'd be cautious about investing too deeply until you see hard results.

My wife and I have experimented with Facebook and found a very low payoff in bookings for a lot of time spent. I would go further and say it currently is a low value-add use of your time. You will certainly get bookings from your loyalty newsletter, but you just might get the odd booking from Facebook.

All around the world folks spend a huge amount of time on Facebook and love it as a distraction from other things in life.

However, a person has many conversations about lots of things that appear briefly for some of their Facebook friends to see. **To get a booking, someone must rave about your place and someone else needs to be thinking about a holiday and see the post in its 90-minute half-life.** Mathematically, these are not good odds. The same goes for Instagram and Twitter.

Given the reassessment of Facebook after the 2016 US election, and the drop in trust for it, society's values are shifting, and the social media giants will try to adapt to these shifts. Where it will lead is unknown. We in the VR industry just need to keep a watching brief before jumping in.

If you enjoy spending lots of time on Facebook, you are there anyway, so why not promote your VR there and run lots of experiments.

On the other hand, don't feel you need to spend a big chunk of time on social media just in case it works. If you spend extra time on social media, what are you going to spend less time on? Whatever you do, don't just add social media to your list and spend more hours on your VR. Some people burn out and abandon their VR because they take on too much.

Although I am negative toward social media as a reliable source of bookings right now, that could change, and I have an open mind.

It will pay to periodically test the water with others to check if it's working consistently or if there are shifts. For example, in 2018, there seems to be a surge in Instagram activity related to VRs. Mastermind groups, conferences, and networking can be very helpful in scanning others to check for success.

If you use social media successfully to get a lot of bookings, please tell me your story—email rex@holidayrentalmastery.com.

Social media and SEO

There is considerable advice from SEO experts that social media activity can be used by Google as a secondary indicator of website authority, and therefore social media can help your SEO. Again, effects seem secondary, and it is a hard ask for a small VR owner to invest heavily for longer-term benefits. For property managers managing many properties at scale, the longer-term investment may be worthwhile and small per property managed.

> Key takeaway: it may be best to wait and observe before jumping in deep with social media, unless you are using it personally anyway.

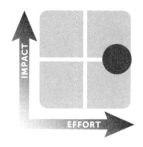

CHAPTER 49

Facebook Ads

> **KEY POINTS**
> - Facebook ads may be valuable for managers of large numbers of VRs, who can spread costs over a large base.
> - For small VR owners, the results aren't clear, so it makes sense to watch and wait for clear results.

There have been promising reports about the effectiveness of Facebook ads, but at the time of writing (2018) it's too early to say just how effective Facebook ads are. The advantage of Facebook ads is that they can be targeted to groups of people:

- Ads can be targeted to groups that match your existing guest market, e.g. young women in a relationship living within several hours of your rental.
- Ads can also be sent to your past guests. You send their email addresses to Facebook so it can find if they are on Facebook, then form a targeted group internally inside the Facebook ad system, then expose them to your ads.
- Facebook can also use that group to construct a similar group, much larger but based on similar characteristics.
- Facebook can also use a retargeting pixel located on your website, to form another group and to send your ads to that group as well.

The advertising software for Facebook ads is well constructed, but like everything else, it takes time to learn, and the interface is constantly changing. For owners of 5–10 VR properties it would be worth the investment of time in a trial for your market. You might even engage a consultant to do it for you.

For owners of just a couple of VR properties, Facebook ads are unlikely to be worth your time, unless you find learning new tools a rewarding adventure.

It's fair to say that you should keep your mind open and periodically scan for reports from thought leaders on the payoff from Facebook ads. If good evidence of effectiveness emerges, you might want to jump in and go for it or employ a consultant to help you. Now it is too early to say.

> **Key takeaway: for small VR owners, the results aren't clear, so it makes sense to watch and wait for clear results.**

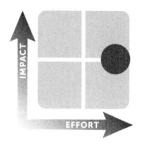

CHAPTER 50

Channel Managers

> **KEY POINTS**
> - Channel manager software allows you to change prices and block out calendars across multiple online travel agencies easily.
> - They are essential for large-scale VRs but are usually not worth the setup effort and cost for small operators.

A channel manager is some software that enables you to control pricing calendar availability and bookings across many online travel agencies.

For our readers

This book is targeted at small VR operators with one to three properties and a handful of online travel agency listings, using simple systems. For most of our readers, a channel manager is just another point of complexity and cost that is not worth the effort. However, they are worth understanding.

Let's say you are listed on four online travel agencies and you get a booking. In a manual world you need to go to the back end of each online travel agency and block out the dates to stop getting another booking for the same dates. You need to do that promptly and exactly right to avoid double bookings. That is triply important if you have "instant booking" turned on.

It can take 2–15 minutes to block out some dates, and it can interrupt your day somewhat, but it can take literally hours and days to untangle double bookings!

Now if you have a channel manager and you take a booking, you can go to just one place and adjust all the calendars for all your online travel agencies with the click of a few buttons. For some software, it can all be done automatically while you sleep. A booking in one OTA is registered in your channel manager, and it blocks out the dates in all the other OTA calendars without your intervention.

CHANNEL MANAGER OPERATION

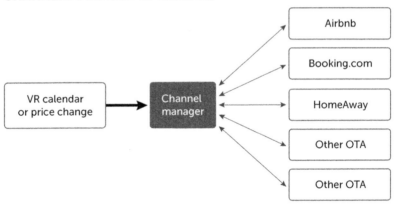

Or so it goes in theory. In past years the reality has been a bit different in that not all online travel agencies have an interface to a common channel manager, and two-way changes are not possible for all OTAs, so exceptions have had to be handled manually.

Also, some updates have a delay of several hours, exposing the VR owner to a double booking in the meantime. That is gradually changing, and more and more OTAs work well both ways with a number of channel managers.

Cost and scale

The SiteMinder channel manager link costs around US$75/mo. for 1–15 rooms (2018): www.siteminder.com/pricing.

As the scale of VR properties and rooms increase, the channel manager comes into its own and is definitely worthwhile. For hotel operators with scores or more rooms operating on a score of online travel agencies, a channel manager integrated into a booking system is crucial. It also allows quick changes in pricing across all the OTAs if the season becomes unexpectedly busy or quiet.

You may have searched for a particular hotel and its own website, only to find their offering on dozens of distribution websites. That hotel is using a channel manager.

If your business scales up to many rooms and many OTAs, definitely use a channel manager.

The practical solution for small VR owners

So how does a small VR operator block out dates across a handful of online travel agency listings? As I described earlier, you can bookmark all your calendar backend logins with saved passwords, open them simultaneously and manually block all the calendars in under three minutes. I've done it thousands of times for the four calendars I use. Easy.

> **Key takeaway: channel managers are essential for large-scale VRs but are usually not worth the setup effort and cost for small operators.**

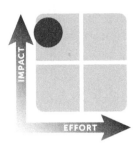

CHAPTER 51

Tips And Hacks

KEY POINTS

- A chapter of handy ideas—like the seven different ways to arrange keys for entry.
- Energy costs can be high—four creative methods are presented to minimize guest energy costs.
- Several hacks to give your guests telephone and internet when the usual channels are unavailable.
- Ways to make your guest's stay easier by fixing discreet labels at the point of use.
- Options for operating your VR remotely while you travel.
- Money-back guarantee, gift vouchers and logo tips.

This section is for those small practical tips that don't necessarily belong in their own section but can help your VR run better.

Managing entry

Where there is just one property with one entry, a keylock is the simple way for your guests to get the key anytime and let themselves in. That is, an openable box with a combination to open and the key within. You can increase security by changing the combination for each guest, typically setting the combination to the last four digits of the guest's mobile—a number they can easily remember.

I used that method in our city townhouse very successfully. The first time setting the combination, the cleaner was flustered with another thing to learn, but a few weeks later she did it in seconds and confided that she enjoyed it!

Another option is to fit an electronic front door lock. Another cost to install, but it can be programmed remotely without intervention by your cleaner. I like to keep it simple and gravitate to a keylock.

For apartment blocks with a single secure entry, there is another challenge—how does the guest get the key? Time for creativity: there is no easy answer. Some owners personally wait at an appointed time for the guest, or use a paid greeting service, which can get messy if the guest is late.

Sometimes there is an all-hours shop that can hand over the key. Once we picked up a key from a left luggage service in Sweden—the guest quotes a number, the service hands over an envelope with the key. In another location the mailboxes were outside, and the owner left the key in the unlocked letterbox. In another location, lockboxes are attached to parking poles on a chain. No easy solutions!

Managing energy use

There is nothing more frustrating than when the guest leaves the heater on (aircon on) and the doors and windows open.

The direct approach is to leave a small note at the heat control requesting responsible energy use and consideration of the environment. If this is a big cost issue, and sometimes it is, you can use the power of the crowd (Psychology chapter) when you speak with the guest: "We are fortunate here that most of our guests are responsible with energy usage. I heard a horror story where another property had a guest who left the heater on with the windows open ..."

Sometimes you need to write a clause in your conditions that says exceptional energy use will attract a fee. Once I came to check that all was well for a 30-day booking for our Richmond house. I noticed that the energy meter was spinning furiously, and the doors and windows were open. I mentioned it to the guest, who said, "Oh, yes, I just like it that way." I explained that the conditions she had accepted that we could bill for additional energy more than 30% above the average guest energy cost. "That's okay," she said. Mom, who was paying for the rental, was a celebrity millionaire, and she paid for the extra energy usage without delay!

Another solution is to install remote energy control and monitoring for temperature and energy. It is initially expensive, but for energy intensive areas like ski chalets, it can be a good investment.

Moderating the use of firewood

I naively thought to help guests by putting a huge stack of firewood at the front door at our Treetops VR to make it easy for guests to load up the wood fireplace. It was *too* easy, and some guests loaded up the fire to use all the wood, with doors and windows open.

After a few experiments, the solution was to just leave the main stack 50 meters away as the only source, so guests only took wood if they really needed it. Usage immediately dropped to sensible levels, and the guest reviews stayed at perfect fives.

Limited communications and internet

Sometimes your VR is in an area with limited mobile and internet coverage, as in Wye River. When figuring out how to handle the problem for guests, I thought back to my meeting with Matt Landau in Panama. I'd stayed at his VR and was given a loan phone on arrival because most guests' mobiles didn't work locally.

I just copied Matt's solution, so I ensured guests at one of our VRs were automatically given a loan mobile if their carrier wasn't the local carrier.

There was a similar but worse problem with internet—there was no ADSL, just wireless data for mobiles on plans. Other VR owners just told their guests no internet was available.

I bought a wireless hotspot dongle, made some simple instructions with a considerable free data allowance. It was in a box with a combination, only those requesting the combination could access it, and to get the password they had to read about their data allowance and the liability to pay for excess data usage. It worked like a charm!

During the life-threatening bushfire that later engulfed our town, our guests were armed with a loan mobile and a data hotspot dongle. They monitored conditions and were ready for my call as the fire broke out of the forest. Warned early, they left early and made it to safety without a problem.

Of course, the loan mobile and the wi-fi hotspot were part of our marketing flaunting the 35 free extras that our guests enjoy— referred to in the earlier Customer Obsession chapter.

These days, good internet reception is essential. Smart VR owners will do what it takes to get good internet coverage for their guests, even if means satellite.

When staying at Lord Howe Island, our first accommodation didn't provide internet, despite offering it on their website. We stayed for a few days and just moved to a more expensive VR that had excellent internet coverage. The cost involved at the time was irrelevant compared to our needs. Of course, I also left a few public reviews behind for others to see the reality.

Running smoothly—good information at the point of use

You will find that guests just want things to work easily without having to contact the owner. You can help them with an information folder referred to in Chapter 16: A Great Guest Experience. You can also help them by using discreetly located notes at the point of use. Tiny labels on light switches are a simple way to help make your guests' stay painless.

Small labelers for discreet messages

I have a Brother labeler that gets used a lot to place discreet signs at points needed. I don't use big intrusive A4 signs, which are bad taste and unprofessional. Instead, small labels are stuck next to the point of use to give the minimum amount of information and guide the guest on how to use the appliance, etc. The Brother label tape is UV-stable, which is why it works better than other brands.

Some examples where I have used labels:

- identifying the boiling water tap
- at the top fridge saying another fridge is downstairs
- at the toilet warning that plastics, etc., down the toilet will block the system and involve a hefty tradesperson's bill
- in the wardrobe showing spare linen is for guest use
- and many, many more.

Laminating

You can also buy an inexpensive laminator to laminate larger signs where it makes sense. I have an A4 laminated guide for setting the wood fire for town guests not familiar with them. "The 100% effective method of setting your fire." It is located with the kindling at the fireplace and stays stiff and clean despite the dust and debris.

You can also make small laminated notes and diagrams and fix them close to where you need the message.

Laminated instructions at the washing machine will last, while a paper version will be ruined with water.

Departure instructions

Heather Bayer, in her excellent podcast, passed on a great tip for instructions for departing guests. Put a laminated sign on the inside of a kitchen cupboard that everyone uses so they can't miss it. Include just the main two or three things you want guests to do when departing, e.g. "When leaving, please put trash in the outside bins and aircon off."

Don't overdo it, if you give them a long list of cleaning jobs, they won't be back—nor should they!

Remote operation of your VR

One of the benefits of getting your VR operation running smoothly with a good cleaner is you can run it from anywhere that has internet access. You can take bookings and communicate with guests anywhere in the world.

When I go on holiday, nothing changes apart from some time zone adjustments. I make sure I buy a local SIM card so I get fast internet while I'm out anywhere. I've taken bookings from all over the world without the guests even knowing where I was.

One challenge was when I had to slip out of a jazz performance in New York to get internet coverage to speak with a prospective Australian guest on Skype, and of course he booked. The jazz performance was still in full swing when I returned. Another challenge was in Greenland with no mobile coverage, where I became a regular visitor to the hotel wi-fi room.

This is not for everyone, and a friend with four VRs chooses to block out all bookings for six weeks and relax completely while he takes his annual holiday. The main point here is that you have the choice to continue operating remotely.

Money-back guarantee

One member of our mastermind group offers a money-back guarantee for guests' satisfaction. He uses the guarantee at the booking stage successfully for the undecided folks and has only been asked for money back once in over a thousand bookings.

On the other hand, he is so customer-focused he will offer a partial refund for the smallest problem, unasked. His guests are happy and give him lots of referrals.

Gift vouchers

Sometimes guests will so enjoy their stay that they want to share the same experience with family or friends as a gift.

Excellent—your job is just to make it easy for them. You should be ready with your Gift Voucher page on your website and a gift voucher link on your home page. You can have an example gift voucher so they can see what they will be giving, along with how to arrange it—just call or email you.

You can promote the gift voucher idea in your newsletter close to Christmas, when people are scratching their heads for a suitable gift. I have one family that gives each of their two children a gift voucher for Christmas every year, and everyone loves it.

Every now and then a team of colleagues are looking for a present for a workmate getting married—you have an easy solution for them. You can see an example of a gift voucher on Seazen.com.au, with a button linking to it on the home page.

Getting a logo

You shouldn't spend attention on a logo until you have achieved high occupancy, but then you can afford the distraction—and give yourself a professional look.

I used 99designs.com to take our rough ideas to a very professional logo in under a week. You present your rough ideas and your needs to the creators on the website, some come back with competing ideas, you shortlist a few, and ask them to modify their ideas in a certain direction. You pay the successful creator. It is highly effective and fun.

Key takeaway: a chapter of handy tips to help run your VR

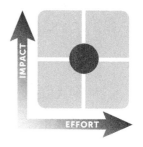

CHAPTER 52

The Advanced Quiz

Item	Implementation question	In place? Yes/Part/No
Conversion tactics	Can you rely on your cleaners to do same-day changeover cleans?	
	Do you have tactics to fill gaps in your calendar? Offers to last-minute email list, offers to extend existing bookings?	
Stand out	Do you clearly create a point of difference from competitors?	
	Do you have an underlying theme for your VR that is different to competitors'?	
	Is your VR name distinctive and easily remembered?	
Loyalty	Do you give special benefits to past guests when returning?	
	Do you capture and record all past guest email addresses?	
	Do you ask guests to refer you to their friends?	
	Do you have branded mementos for guests to take home?	

Item	Implementation question	In place? Yes/Part/ No
Email marketing	Do you send email newsletters to past guests, at least four times per year?	
	Do you use email marketing software for newsletters?	
Own website	Do you have your own website?	
	Can your guests access your calendar from your website?	
	Can you edit your own website pages?	
Online booking	Can guests book online via your website?	
	Can you take card bookings manually?	
Google My Business	Is your VR listed on Google My Business?	
Feedback obsession	Do you ask guests during booking how they found you?	
	Do you ask guests after their stay for feedback, either written or by phone?	
	Do you have a guest book inside your VR?	
Reviews	Do you personally ask guest to leave you a review?	
	Do you have a steady flow of reviews on your website and online travel agencies?	

Item	Implementation question	In place? Yes/Part/ No
Pricing	Is pricing up-to-date, accurate, and adjusted for seasonal peaks?	
	Do you benchmark your prices against your competition at least once per year?	
Insider's guide	Do you have a professional-looking guide with your personal recommendations for guests for local food and experiences?	
Google Ads	Are you aware of the benefits and risks of Google Ads for your VR?	
Mastermind	Do you have a group of colleagues with whom you share learning about VRs in your local area?	
Knowledge	Do you subscribe to newsletters and/or podcasts to keep up-to-date with latest trends in the VR industry?	
	Do you attend workshops or conferences related to the VR industry?	
Publicity	Do you have media coverage of your VR?	
Social media	Are you aware of the effort vs bookings trade-off from social media?	
Facebook ads	Are you aware of the benefits and risks of Facebook ads?	
Channel manager	Are you aware of the benefits and risks of channel managers?	
Offline marketing	Do you explore and exploit offline marketing opportunities?	

Item	Implementation question	In place? Yes/Part/ No
Other	Is your floor plan shown on your websites?	
	Do you have a video tour visible on your website?	
	Is your booking occupancy 70% or greater all year round?	
Add up the number of yes answers (Only include Yes, not Part or No answers)		

HOW DID YOU SCORE?

Your score out of 37 questions	Where you stand on the advanced methods
0–19	You are starting on your journey
20–27	Very good progress
28–37	Outstanding—on the path to mastery

CHAPTER 53

Conclusion— Continuing The Journey

This is not a one-shot project but rather a journey over time, where persistence and patience pay off. Over time, experience will give you wisdom. Over time, your loyal guests will grow to be raving fans and your occupancy and profitability will grow.

Along the way it will be a personally rewarding experience as you continue to bring happiness to folks on vacation.

Enjoy the journey!

Our contribution

For knowledge and nourishment on the journey, visit www.holidayrentalmastery.com and subscribe to my newsletter.

References

Brown, Rex. 2014. "It's A cleaning Business." Holiday Rental Mastery. www.holidayrentalmastery.com/its-a-cleaning-business

Business Wire. 2017. "Global Vacation Rental Market To Be Worth USD 193.89 Billion By 2021: Technavio." Last modified February 16, 2017. www.businesswire.com/news/home/20170216005440/en/Global-Vacation-Rental-Market-Worth-USD-193.89

Hinote, Amy. 2015. "The Changing Landscape Of Third Party Booking Channels." *VRM Intel*, October 2015. https://issuu.com/vrmintel/docs/vrm_intel_magazine_oct_2015_issuu/45?e=19363421/31068452

HomeAway. 2018. "Travel Hack: New HomeAway Data Reveals The Best Time To Book Vacations." Last modified January 19, 2018. www.homeaway.com/info/media-center/press-releases/PR_2018/travel-hack-new-homeaway-data-reveals-the-best-time-to-book-vaca

Jones, January. 2018. "Airbnb Repositions, Unveils Plus, Beyond And Collections To Broaden Its Options." *Domain*, February 23, 2018. www.domain.com.au/news/airbnb-repositions-unveils-plus-beyond-and-collections-to-broaden-its-options-20180223-h0win9/

Kahneman, Daniel. 2010. "The Riddle Of Experience Vs. Memory." www.conferences.ted.com/TED2010/program/

MarketScreener. 2018. Google's financial details. Last modified October 24, 2018. www.4-traders.com/GOOGLE-INC-9469/financials/

McLeod, Betsy. 2018. "61 Mobile Marketing Statistics For 2018 And Beyond." Last modified April 6, 2018. www.bluecorona.com/blog/mobile-marketing-statistics

Nielsen. 2009. "Global Advertising Consumers Trust Real Friends And Virtual Strangers The Most." Last modified on July 7, 2009. www.nielsen.com/us/en/insights/news/2009/global-advertising-consumers-trust-real-friends-and-virtual-strangers-the-most.html

Schaal, Dennis. 2018. "Booking Claims It Beats Airbnb With 5 million Alternative Accommodations Listings." Last modified April 10, 2018. www.skift.com/2018/04/10/booking-claims-it-beats-airbnb-with-5-million-alternative-accommodations-listings/

Shakespeare, Stephan. 2016. "Airbnb Books Place Among Young Savvy Travellers." Last modified May 11, 2016. www.cityam.com/240806/airbnb-books-place-among-young-savvy-travellers

Sundaresan, Bindu. 2018. "Danny Meyer, when and how to ignore conventional wisdom." Last modified October 23, 2018. www.mastersofscale.com/#/danny-meyer-when-and-how-to-ignore-conventional-wisdom/

Ting, Deanna. 2017. "Airbnb Growth Story Has A Plot Twist— A Saturation Point." Last modified November 15, 2017. www.skift.com/2017/11/15/airbnb-growth-story-has-a-plot-twist-a-saturation-point/

Wikipedia. 2018. 'WordPress." Last modified October 21, 2018. www.en.wikipedia.org/wiki/WordPress

Printed in Great Britain
by Amazon

78584093R00167